ESSENTIALS
of Enterprise Compliance

ESSENTIALS
of Enterprise Compliance

Susan D. Conway, Ph.D., PMP
Mara E. Conway, JD, LLM

WILEY

John Wiley & Sons. Inc.

This book is printed on acid-free paper. ⊚

Copyright © 2008 by John Wiley & Sons, Inc. All rights reserved.

Published by John Wiley & Sons, Inc., Hoboken, New Jersey.

Published simultaneously in Canada.

For general information on our other products and services, or technical support, please contact our Customer Care Department within the United States at 800-762-2974, outside the United States at 317-572-3993 or fax 317-572-4002.

Wiley also publishes its books in a variety of electronic formats. Some content that appears in print may not be available in electronic books.

For more information about Wiley products, visit our Web site at http://*www.wiley.com*.

Library of Congress Cataloging-in-Publication Data:

Conway, Susan, 1947-
   Essentials of enterprise compliance / Susan D. Conway, Mara E. Conway.
      p.   cm.
   Includes index.
   ISBN 978-0-470-40476-8 (pbk.)
      1. Corporate governance.   2. Business enterprises—Law and legislation.   3. Business ethics.
   I. Conway, Mara E., 1970-   II. Title.
   HD2741.C696   2008
   658.1'2—dc22
                                                                    2008019301

Printed in the United States of America

10 9 8 7 6 5 4 3 2 1

Contents

Preface

This book is written in such a way to address the key business issues around enterprise compliance while highlighting real-world legal issues and discussions. Enterprise compliance has been broken down into four key components: governance, compliance, workforce migration, and technology support, as shown in Exhibit A.

Content Road Map★

	Governance	Compliance	Workforce Migration	Technology Support
Part I Introduction	G	{C	WM}	T
Part II Framework for Governance	G	{C	WM}	T
Part III Looking For the High Ground	G	{C	WM}	

*Brackets indicate that discussion is grouped together.

As Exhibit A demonstrates, the legal and regulatory challenges facing business in the twenty-first century are best addressed based on the level at which they are executed. Compliance and workforce migration (immigration and related employment law issues) are both addressed at the operational level, whereas governance is an executive- and board-level issue. Though all three concepts will be addressed in Parts I and II, governance will be treated uniquely while compliance and migration discussions can be joined. We will have an opportunity to discuss all three in unison in Part III as we look forward.

Technology is an enabler of all aspects of enterprise compliance. Potential technology benefits and risks will be discussed in Parts I and II.

Foreword

From the board of directors and executives to the general management and sales representatives, no one can act as passive, or even limited, advisers to the enterprise they serve. Members of corporate boards must take an increasingly active role in fulfilling their fiduciary responsibilities of oversight. They are no longer "window dressing," and they should act effectively to add value to the company. Executive leadership must proactively engage in the dissemination of guidance, and their managers must actively work to structure compliance within the rank and file. Corporate governance has gone from being something "nice to do" to "please a few investors" to an essential component of a company's valuation and risk assessment processes.

Although some organizations see compliance as a burden, others see it as an opportunity. Forward-thinking chief financial officers (CFOs) are structuring their governance policies, processes, and controls to enhance and reinforce long-term compliance.[1] They plan not only to meet today's compliance needs but to go beyond them, and in doing so they create genuine competitive advantages for their organizations.

These visionaries view regulatory compliance as a catalyst for change. This view can be contrasted with other business leaders who spend their time and resources in a reactive tactical effort to simply address today's audit or legal challenges. A study by IDC[2] found that the average company with revenue over $1 billion spends an average of $3.70 million annually to meet their Sarbanes-Oxley requirements. These CFOs tend to view legislation like Basel[3] II as a "tax"—an unavoidable and incremental finance cost. They seem to hope that it will soon pass.

> Moving compliance from overhead to business as usual is the new productivity frontier.

Forward-thinking business and government leaders are seeking out means to strengthen their compliance activities while working to offset the incremental cost of compliance. They recognize this as an opportunity to partner with other areas of the business to lower operating costs and improve business performance by streamlining processes, standardizing reporting, and integrating technologies, while delivering the organization's compliance status at any time.

Competitive advantage is achieved through benefit-driven activities that embed compliance in the "business as usual" operations of an organization, creating a transformational journey from compliance to competitive advantage. *Essentials of Enterprise Compliance* focuses on this journey. Though each journey has common components, it is also unique to each enterprise. Regardless of law and regulation, the specific governance and compliance structure is guided by the unique culture, business processes, information management, and enabling information technology (IT) of the enterprise. These unique factors underscore the transformational benefits required to be competitive and deliver tangible savings and returns through compliance transformation.

Microsoft believes that to achieve the competitive advantage journey vision, an organization should have technologies that enable its people and become "People Ready." Delivered through its enabling IT, the technologies must be scalable, security enhanced, and, above all, intuitive to the people within the organization.

Discovering solutions that meet the vision for competitive advantage and compliance requirements, and that enable the forward motion of the enterprise, should be the joint vision of all parties. Isn't it time you considered leveraging your investment and delivering tangible results?

Mike McDuffie

Vice President, Public Sector, Microsoft Corporation

Notes

1. CFO Research Services in collaboration with Capgemini, "Compliance: Finance's Bridge to the Enterprise," 2005.

2. IDC/Revenue Recognition.com, Financial executive benchmarking panel survey, SOX edition, 2005.

3. The Basel Accord (I and II) refers to the European based banking supervision agreements and is regulated by the Basel Committee on Banking Supervision (BCBS) based in Basel, Switzerland.

PART I

Introduction

After reading this book, you will be able to:

- Appreciate the value of establishing a unified and holistic governance and compliance framework.
- Better understand the relationship between governance and compliance.
- Develop a global vision of enterprise governance and compliance.
- Deepen your understanding of the major terms, concepts, and objectives of enterprise governance and compliance in the public and commercial sectors.

Governance is an expression of the stakeholder vision that serves to guide the operation of the enterprise. Governance policy can be envisioned as the core of a series of interlocking circles that form the foundation of successful enterprise. Compliance, revolving tightly around governance, is linked closely to data, security, quality, operational excellence, and financial transparency, which in turn connects to the broader issues of records and data management, accessibility, and intellectual capital security. You may immediately recognize these as the same relationships as those that are required for successful business management.

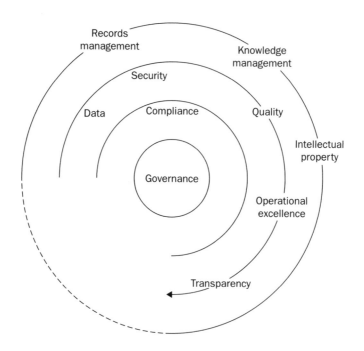

In the information-centric economy, without governance and compliance rules the enterprise would focus solely on the efficient and effective delivery of information without concern for the asset value or security of the deliverable. It is the role of governance policy to set constraints on this flow to secure not only the assets but to preserve the individual and business data privacy rights. Compliance drives this constraint to a granular level through the evolution of business rules that are executed in the operation of the business. Business rules, in turn, dictate the degrees of freedom that can be exercised in the production and use of information, enterprise knowledge, data, and intellectual property. Enterprises that ignore any of these key relationships open themselves to heightened levels of risk, including exposure to legal action, sanctions, and loss of stakeholder confidence.

TIPS AND TECHNIQUES

Focus on Compliance

Few business issues are higher profile than compliance. The number and scope of compliance regulations have increased dramatically over the past few years, making compliance an ever-complex business and technology challenge. Whether aimed to prevent fraud and money laundering, to combat international terrorism, or to ensure financial accountability and privacy, a kaleidoscope of international, federal, and state regulations—such as the USA PATRIOT Act, Sarbanes-Oxley Act (SOX), Basel II, Bank of England, Bank Secrecy Act, Health Insurance Portability and Accountability Act (HIPAA), and others—dramatically impacts how companies do business.

To be successful, organizations serious about compliance must also be serious about process and data quality because at the core of any reliable compliance program is consistent and quality data. Ideally, an organization's compliance framework will provide structured procedures, quality management, and matching staff capabilities as part of an all-encompassing enterprise compliance and case-management solution.

Organizations that have pieced together their compliance process should carefully review its design and audit its results to ensure that the process that has developed over time is up to the task of meeting the company's current requirements. In particular, organizations that plan to use existing management and quality structures for their compliance efforts must carefully examine the ability of such programs to effectively extend rules and processing capabilities in order to provide mission-critical and compliance-specific capabilities, without which the entire compliance process could be undermined.

The last few years have been challenging for those who work to manage these interrelated risks. From corporate scandals such as Enron and WorldCom to data privacy breaches at Choice Point and Bank of America, businesses today are pressed to develop more reliable methods of ensuring, tracking, and recording compliance-related factors involving not only employees and executives but also corporate and customer data.

In a global economy where an instant message from a contractor in Bangalore can throw a Boston-based company out of Sarbanes-Oxley compliance, understanding corporate compliance rules and information technology (IT) policies must be taken to a new level. Information-centric intellectual capital (people, knowledge, and data) has become the core asset of global enterprises. These virtual think factories may have designers working in Britain, engineering based in the United States, and manufacturing in China. This structure results in a complex compliance web enabled by information technology, complex business process outsourcing, and matrix management that is scattered across the organization.[1]

Business leaders and their advisers have been forced to reflect on what it means to have a strong compliance system. What are the components of effective controls? What does it mean to put a focus on corporate compliance and ethics? No enterprise is immune from the risks. Those who follow business news know that nearly every public organization and many private organizations have struggled with litigation exposures, regulatory investigations, and the like. Anytime you have employees spread across the globe in countless countries, you wake up every morning or you fall asleep every night thinking that any one of them can do something just slightly out of line and cause a great deal of peril to the enterprise. The key question is how you protect the enterprise against that in circumstances where you can never entirely eliminate the risk. Things will happen—there will be regulatory challenges, lawsuits, and incidents that cause concern—but the question is how to set up a structure of governance and internalize a set of business rules and values that will minimize the risk and convince the people who work for you and those who do business with you that the standards that govern your enterprise truly matter to you. Corporate governance and compliance should matter as much as meeting the revenue/budget targets, in satisfying the expectations of the business leaders, owners, and the board of directors.

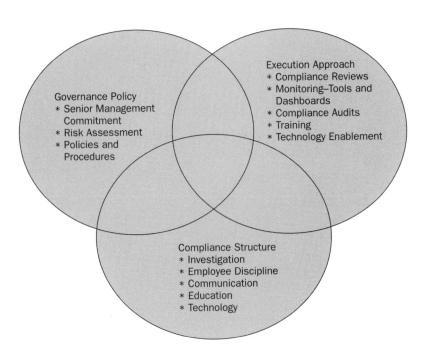

The corporate experiences of recent years, for better or worse, are driving culture change. The new breed of business executive will need a framework for understanding how global labor, IT policies, and international legal compliance influences information work and drives business productivity.

Establishing a culture of compliance requires a continuous cycle of guidance, planning/reporting, and execution/monitoring.

Note

1. Susan Conway, *The Think Factory* (Hoboken, NJ: John Wiley & Sons, 2007).

CHAPTER 1

Compliance: Law and Society

After reading this chapter, you will be able to:

- Understand the basic structure of an enterprise governance framework.
- Deepen your understanding of the relationship between governance and compliance.
- Develop a conceptual foundation for evaluating your enterprise's current governance and compliance program.
- Understand the structure of a holistic governance and compliance framework.
- Appreciate the reasons for unified enterprise framework.
- Review the balance between governance and compliance in public and commercial enterprises.

Defining the Scope

Governance policy and compliance rules can no longer be passive guidance for CEOs, managers, supervisors, and employees. Members of corporate boards must take an increasingly active role in fulfilling their fiduciary responsibilities of oversight with proactive governance structures and compliance frameworks.

As Mike McDuffie pointed out earlier, a board of directors is no longer *window dressing*, and, therefore, must be a contributing factor in establishing solid governance across the enterprise. Organizational compliance rules must proactively implement the governance policy as well as ensure adherence to law. Adding to this complex picture is the organizational culture and operational management of the enterprise. Over the course of this chapter we will explore some of these interdependencies and try to peel back the layers, as shown in Exhibit 1.1, enough to clarify the relationship between governance, compliance, and operations.

Enterprise governance policy is the core of processes, customs, policies, and rules that guides and influences the way in which an organization is directed, administered, or controlled. Governance generally provides guidance on the relationships and a role of the people involved and includes an alignment of the rules to the goals of the enterprise. Enterprise governance is, for the benefit of the stakeholders (shareholders, owners, or citizens), designed to provide guidance from the board of directors, management, and, ultimately, the employees in the proper operation of the enterprise. It is often a set of lofty statements aligned to the enterprise mission and goals.

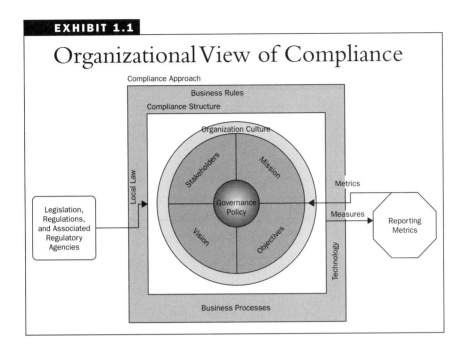

EXHIBIT 1.1

Organizational View of Compliance

Given this definition, it is clear that enterprise governance is not simply an outline for managing external regulations but is a high-level set of guidelines to the complex issue of enterprise operations. The focal point of governance, and its operational counterpart compliance, is accountability and fiduciary duty. The primary objective of governance, as outlined in Exhibit 1.1, is to provide a framework under which compliance is built. Governance, if structured and managed well, provides guidance to the operational processes and supporting systems that lead to good institutional behavior that in turn leads to shareholder protection and economic efficiency. Governance is about the delicate balance between appropriate workplace behavior and economic gains.

Governance Point of View

FROM THE REAL WORLD

Corporate Governance at Merrill Lynch

Merrill Lynch believes that good corporate governance is a critical factor in achieving business success. The board of directors has long adhered to best practices in corporate governance in fulfillment of its responsibilities to shareholders and to oversee the work of management and the company's business.

As we rapidly approach the decade mark of the Enron Corporation collapse, the concept of governance continues to evolve as a key stakeholder tool. Clearly understanding the point of view required in a governance policy is critical to establishing a good policy. Today, the concept of stakeholder theory, as described by Professor R. Edward Freeman (1984), seems to express the leading point of view of governance responsibility. Essentially, Professor Freeman states, it is the responsibility of the enterprise to convert the inputs of investors (owners) into usable (salable) outputs that, in turn, generate benefit (economic profit or social good).[1] Complexity grows as the number of stakeholders in the modern enterprise view has grown to include employees, unions, suppliers, and, today, the public (represented by regulatory agencies and associations). Translating, monitoring, and measuring this equation into a unified policy is challenging. As the board and senior management have become not only morally but also legally responsible for compliance, they are increasingly taking the proactive step of seeking management and technology partners to support, execute, and audit the governance policies and guidelines they set forth.

Starting a Compliance Program

The start of a compliance program often requires an assessment, conducted by auditors, of the legislation and regulations with which the organization must comply, the conflicts between them, and reconciliation with the corporate governance policies.

After this audit, the organization needs to understand how current policies, procedures, and local regulations are affected, and the organization needs to design a benefit-driven strategy to address these points. The organization also needs to understand how the results of the audit affect the technologies the company utilizes and will eventually require.

What decisions and behaviors should be managed for sound governance and compliance? Private- and public-sector businesses face a multi-tiered challenge best described in layers:

To be successful in a compliance-oriented world, a well-run organization should demand a sustainable, benefit-driven approach. Strategic benefits can accrue from a well-designed, holistic compliance strategy. For example, an organization required to meet Sarbanes-Oxley needs to have a robust and controls-based approach, such as Control Objectives for Information and Related Technology (COBIT). A tactical and silo *regulation- and legislation-driven* approach can compromise the future ability of the organization to meet and benefit from compliance initiatives.

EXHIBIT 1.2

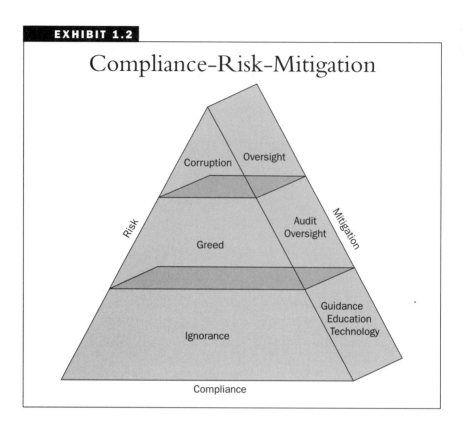

Compliance-Risk-Mitigation

Building a holistic program requires balancing the drivers of compliance with the risks faced by the enterprise and its officers. Understanding the causes of noncompliance, as outlined in Exhibit 1.2—corruption, greed, and ignorance—helps the organization build a risk mitigation plan.

- Ignorance is often the easiest challenge to address and the most complex to implement. The virtual and geographically dispersed workforce presents a challenge to any guidance and education program. The larger the workforce, the more challenging it is to ensure that knowledge is transmitted and understood by all parties. Technology, as we will discuss in Part II, can provide implicit guidance and explicit education.

- *Example:* An employee accidentally gives advance notice of a bid to a vendor, providing unfair advantage.

- Greed requires constant vigilance through audits and monitoring. This form of mitigation gets a great deal of attention in the run-of-the-mill compliance books—written by auditors (of course). Though auditors comment that finding the greedy is not as much a technology challenge as it is a cultural and process issue, we will spend some time examining technology enablers to help management monitor and guard against the greed factor.

  - *Example:* In 1995 Nick Leeson, over a three-month period, used his position with Barings Investment Bank in Singapore to purchase 20,000 futures contracts worth about $180,000 each in a vain attempt to move the market. Some three-quarters of the $1.3 billion he lost Barings resulted from these trades. When Barings executives discovered what had happened, they informed the Bank of England that Barings was effectively broke. In his wake, Nick Leeson had wiped out the 233-year-old Barings Investment Bank. The $1.3 billion dollars of liabilities he had run up was more than the entire capital and reserves of the bank.

- Corruption is probably the most newsworthy of the challenges though not the most common. Guarding against corruption requires consistent and vigilant oversight by the board of directors and company executives. Technology can support the discovery and detection of corruption but certainly is not the front-line defense against these actions. A strong and active board of directors and executives carrying out a well-architected and -monitored governance policy is the best offense.

- *Example:* Global Crossing, like Enron, collapsed into bankruptcy early in 2002, as Representative Felix Grucci (R-NY) stated, due to "absolute, unfettered greed." Charges of deceptive accounting practices and misrepresentation of assets by management demonstrated potential challenges to U.S. accounting practices in general and led to the passage of the Sarbanes-Oxley Act as the U.S. Congress moved to protect shareholder rights from greed in the executive offices.

Structuring Compliance

Compliance, as the granular delivery arm of governance, must address four major aspects to be effective:

1. Culture

2. Governance

3. Information management

4. Processes

Mitigating compliance risk requires, as discussed earlier, a solid governance policy supported by an organizational culture of compliance, along with tools to capture, document, collaborate, and record the processes, actions, and collaboration embedded throughout the environment.

One of the most intriguing complications of the governance/compliance challenge today is the global nature of work. Commercial, nonprofit, and government enterprises need to work locally but think globally. Even enterprises traditionally bound to the local economy, such as farming, find it necessary to consider the global economy when purchasing inventory or hiring workers.

Chapter Summary

Just as a house built on a solid foundation stands the test of time, an enterprise structured on a solid governance policy is well positioned to build an effective and efficient compliance program. It is the duty of the board of directors to ensure that governance policy is designed to address both legal compliance and strategic alignment. The handshake with the compliance program must clearly provide the board with transparency into enterprise operations and an understanding of how the program underscores required practices and fosters a culture of compliance to both regulation and enterprise policy.

Corporate governance provides a framework of checks and balances between the board, management, and investors that should produce an efficiently functioning corporation, geared to produce long-term value. All enterprise governance policies, regardless of country of origin, are the product of the blending of relevant legal, regulatory, and best-practice concepts. Each country's regulatory and corporate law system will shape the specifics of its corporate governance framework.

For example, corporate governance systems in the United States are shaped by a number of pressures including the Securities and Exchange Commission's (SEC's) regulatory oversight, which provides for:

- Stock exchange listing requirements
- Congressional ability to enact wide-sweeping federal legislation

15

- Local influences such as precedents set by the state courts

- The influence of institutional investors, including the power of proxy voting tactics, such as the filing of shareowner proposals

Although all of these influences can help focus attention on critical elements of good governance, they cannot tell corporate directors or officers how to determine whether the board has set appropriate goals for its own operations or whether the board is achieving success in reaching these goals. This portion of governance extends the responsibilities of the board and senior management in the realm of internal risk management.

The global nature of work is today, and will remain in the future, a governance and compliance challenge. A mobile workforce, with an employee in New York today and Peking next year, represents challenges on a number of fronts including personal, legal, human resources, and compliance. The mobile worker must be informed and prepared to comply with the policy and regulations in each new location. The shrinking world of work creates an expanding compliance vista for the enterprise and its workforce.

Note

1. R. Edward Freeman, professor of business administration at Dardem School, University of Virginia, is known for his work in stakeholder theory *(Managing for Stakeholders,* Yale University Press, 2007).

CHAPTER 2

Global Perspective

After reading this chapter, you will be able to:

- Develop a deeper appreciation for the legal foundation and influences of local law on enterprise governance.
- Compare global governance and compliance requirements for multinational enterprises.

Influencing Governance Structures

As the twenty-first century opened, the world seemed to be discovering the impact of globalization on governance. The debate focused on the impact of local government regulation on governance. By 2004, Art Durnev and Kim Han announced to the 14th Annual Conference on Financial Economics and Accounting (FEA) that:

> For many countries in the world, there is relatively little empirical evidence on governance mechanisms other than legal protection and ownership structure. Such issues as board structure, compensation, and changes

in control have been extensively studied in the U.S. but have been studied much less—if at all—for many other world economies. This may reflect the dominant role of ownership structure in these economies, a dominance that appears to be driven at least in part by weaknesses in legal systems. Evolutions in legal structure provide for natural corporate governance experiments. Financial globalization reduces the importance of country characteristics, thereby increasing the incentives for good governance.[1]

In the light of the rapid growth of the intertwined global economy, research into governance structures has been aggressively viewed by researchers, investors, and financial institutions. The trend, by 2006, appeared to be moving toward a common image of governance with the structure of corporate governance being shaped more by ownership than country of origin.[2] A Conference Board study in 2006 has revealed that global corporate governance models do not necessarily vary as much by country (e.g., a U.S. model of corporate governance compared to an Asian or a European model). The ownership model associated with enterprise, regardless of the country or the region it calls home, essentially drives its governance model. Generally, best practices, such as the number of directors, unless moderated by local laws, will differ depending not on location but on a company's key corporate ownership structure, whether it is:

- Widely held and dispersed across many shareholders;
- An enterprise that is closely held by blocks of investors;
- A family-owned business;
- A newly privatized business where the government retains a residual investment; or
- A government or nonprofit agency.

As an enterprise's ownership structure changes or matures, its governance practices will change. Policy will be shaped to reflect the current stage of development (e.g., founding company versus mature company), formal structure, and the leadership styles of senior management and the board.[3] Policy changes are first seen in the annual update by the board of directors or organizational leadership, which reflects the changes in ownership, laws, and regulations.

Public faith in corporate governance was shaken by the catastrophic failures of Enron, WorldCom, and other companies, and has been slow to recover. These failures uncovered a number of process gaps that companies cannot allow in the future. Establishing and structuring corporate governance practices is now an essential part of an organization's risk management plan and something boards and directors cannot afford to overlook. Boards should provide oversight and encourage management to assess and manage risk and provide internal efficiencies in running the corporation, while ensuring growth.

Governance policy for public agencies takes guidance from a different set of legislation but is driven in a similar manner. In the United States, congressional guidance in the form of legislation such as the Clinger-Cohen Act (CCA)[4] and the later E-Government Act (2002), along with oversight agencies such as the Office of Management and Budget (OMB), provides public agencies with guidance on managing electronic data, while the National Archives and Records Administration (NARA) seeks to guide policy on data retention and records management. Governance in the public sector is more focused on information security while allowing appropriate transparency and providing for a satisfactory level of public oversight into the operations of the government.

The enactment of the CCA (1996), the Sarbanes–Oxley Act in 2002 (SOX), and the Committee of Sponsoring Organizations of the Treadway Commission (COSO), along with related regulatory acts by agencies such as the SEC and OMB, provide a more rigorous framework for a whole host of corporate governance and federally mandated internal control reforms in the United States and around the world. (See Appendix A for additional discussion on this issue.)

FROM THE REAL WORLD

Managing Stakeholder Risk Is a Key Component of Governance

The following excerpt shows how financial institutions must constantly manage their risk exposure:

The Bank of England is growing increasingly concerned at large inflows of money into hedge funds as institutions and individuals are prepared to take higher risks than in the past in pursuit of high investment returns.

Releasing its twice-yearly financial stability review, the Bank said the British and international financial systems are currently relatively benign and near-term risks are low.

But this could be storing up problems, the Bank said. "In the present benign environment, there is a possibility that lenders, borrowers, and investors may be inclined to under estimate long-run vulnerabilities and take on too much risk," said Sir Andrew Large, the Bank's deputy governor responsible for financial stability. The review was also worried about the rapid growth of unsecured, or non-mortgaged, borrowing in Britain. It said while banks had improved their credit-scoring models and so-called "stress tests," a period of economic downturn may lead to lenders making it more difficult for borrowers to roll over their unsecured loans and cause wider repayment problems.

Ashley Seager, *The Guardian*, Monday, December 13, 2004; www.guardian.co.uk

Thinking Global Compliance

The complexity driven by multiple sets of laws and regulations continues to drive global enterprises to lobby for legislative changes in their home countries, thus often causing a chain reaction of changes around the globe. The chain reaction caused by the collapse of Enron, WorldCom, and Global Crossing caused reactionary changes in corporate regulations around the world. The financial markets reacted to downfalls in the banking system, such as the downfall of Barings in 1995 and more recently Northern Rock (2207) in the United Kingdom, resulting in Basel II rules being more strictly enforced throughout the European Union (EU), as well as the enactment of similar regulations in other parts of the world.

Compliance frameworks are built on the twin drivers of enterprise governance and local law. The global information-centric economy has given the image of a global economy, but it is imperative to remember that law is still a local matter. Though we will spend a few more pages comparing global legislation and regulations, the primary focus of our discussion is intended to go beyond what is required by law and capture best practices for internal governance and compliance improvement. In short, our goal is to help business and government leaders develop a framework for successful governance and compliance environments.

United States—Compliance Notes

Compliance for U.S. corporations is generally interpreted to mean compliance with federal laws and regulations. There are criminal and/or civil penalties associated with violation of the various laws and regulations. Compliance planning is loosely defined and generally left to the boards of directors under the governance policies of the companies. The general reference for most compliance plans comes from the U.S. sentencing guidelines in Chapter 8 of the Federal Sentencing Guidelines.[5]

In 2002, the Sarbanes-Oxley Act (named for sponsors Senator Paul Sarbanes and Representative Michael Oxley) defined tighter personal responsibility codes for top corporate management regarding the accuracy of financial statements.

Although the Sarbanes-Oxley Act (SOX) consists of 11 major titles and numerous sections, four of them directly influence information technology (IT): Sections 302, 404, 409, and 1102. Sections 307, 407, and 907 combined outline the compliance, reporting, and penalties related to the legislation, while Sections 302, 407, and 409 are particularly compelling for top-level management:

- **Section 302** requires that CEOs/CFOs assure the accuracy of financial reports and guarantee that the data used to compile these reports is correct and has not been manipulated in any way. Because those financial reports are produced using a company's IT systems, the security and integrity of those systems is a fundamental requirement.

- **Section 407** is divided into two focus areas and has the greatest impact on the IT department. In fact, the majority of money companies spend on compliance is linked to meeting Section 407.

  - **Part (a)** requires that each annual report include an "internal control report" indicating that management is responsible for an adequate internal control structure and an assessment of its effectiveness. Any shortcomings or material weaknesses in these controls must be reported.

  - **Part (b)** requires that an external auditor attest to, and report on, management's assertions regarding its assessment of the effectiveness of the company's internal controls.

- **Section 409** requires companies to disclose, on a rapid and current basis (48 hours), information concerning material changes in its financial condition or operations.

 TIPS AND TECHNIQUES

Penalties

Section 1102 imparts penalties for anyone who tampers with a record, document, or other object with the intent to impair the object's integrity or availability for use in an official proceeding.

(continued)

23

Section 906 modified the U.S. Criminal Code to require each period filing by companies regulated under the Exchange Act to include a financial statement. The false certification by a chief executive officer and/or a chief financial officer of a company, under this provision, can be subject to criminal prosecution. Penalties for false certification include fines ranging from $1 million to $5 million and prison sentences of 10 to 20 years, depending on the violation.

Though publicly held businesses receive most of the attention in the press, privately held enterprises, large or small, are also subject to external rules and regulations. However, many of the SEC reporting rules do not apply to these enterprises; corruption and employment/tax–related reporting rules are still considerable and must be factored in as part of the risk within the management and operating environment.

> About three quarters of all U.S. business firms have no payroll. Most are self-employed persons operating unincorporated businesses, and may or may not be the owner's principal source of income. Because nonemployers account for only about 3.4 percent of business receipts, they are not included in most business statistics, for example, most reports from the Economic Census. Since 1997, however, nonemployers have grown faster than employer firms.[6]

The U.S. Small Business Administration (SBA) maintains an extensive web site[7] to provide resources for business owners to access government services and information that can be helpful in building good compliance plans (see Exhibits 2.1 and 2.2).

EXHIBIT 2.1

Employers and Nonemployers, 2002 (U.S. SBA)

	Firms	# Establishments	Sales or Receipts ($1,000)
All firms	23,343,821	24,846,832	22,832,560,524
Nonemployers (firms with no payroll)	17,646,062	17,646,062	770,032,328
Employers (firms with payroll)	5,697,759	7,200,770	22,062,528,196

Other than the widely talked about Sarbanes-Oxley Act, other regulations including in banking and financial services the Gramm-Leach-Bliley Act (GLBA[8]), Federal Information Security Management Act of 2002 (FISMA[9]), and Health Insurance Portability and Accountability Act (HIPAA[10]) exist to provide regulations regarding operation in various industries and enterprises. Frameworks such as the Canadian Institute of Chartered Accountants' Criteria of Control Board (COCO), Control Objectives for Information and Related Technology (COBIT[11]) and standards such as the National Institute of Standards and Technology (NIST[12]) inform organizations on how to comply with the regulations.

Life sciences businesses have been affected in the past decade by increased competition and pressure to operate in a more closely regulated environment. As a result, pharmaceutical and biotechnology companies face the need to establish better integration and standardized processes across their organizations. Complying with these

Employment Size of Employer and Nonemployer Firms, 2004 (U.S. SBA)

Employment Size of Enterprise	Firms	# Establishments	Paid Employees	Annual Payroll ($1,000)	Sales or Receipts ($1,000)
All firms	**25,409,525**	**26,911,465**	**115,074,924**	**4,253,995,732**	**N/A**
Nonemployer firms	19,523,741	19,523,741	N/A	N/A	887,001,820
Employer firms	**5,885,784**	**7,387,724**	**115,074,924**	**4,253,995,732**	**N/A**
Firms with no employees as of March 12, but with payroll at some time during the year	802,034	803,355	0	40,043,549	N/A
Firms with 1 to 4 employees	2,777,680	2,782,252	5,844,637	165,904,564	N/A
Firms with 5 to 9 employees	1,043,448	1,055,937	6,852,769	195,519,100	N/A
Firms with 10 to 19 employees	632,682	666,574	8,499,681	257,802,789	N/A
Firms with 20 to 99 employees	526,355	692,677	20,642,614	670,418,442	N/A
Firms with 100 to 499 employees	86,538	330,447	16,757,751	587,676,161	N/A
Firms with 500 employees or more	17,047	1,056,482	56,477,472	2,336,631,127	N/A
Firms with 500 to 749 employees	5,695	66,305	3,449,491	130,408,281	N/A
Firms with 750 to 999 employees	2,709	41,835	2,331,851	87,180,964	N/A
Firms with 1,000 to 1,499 employees	2,828	57,479	3,444,427	132,832,629	N/A
Firms with 1,500 to 2,499 employees	2,281	76,491	4,396,430	179,582,908	N/A
Firms with 2,500 employees or more	3,534	814,372	42,855,273	1,806,626,345	N/A
Firms with 2,500 to 4,999 employees	1,739	106,893	6,038,196	262,111,452	N/A
Firms with 5,000 to 9,999 employees	905	120,311	6,378,292	278,396,903	N/A
Firms with 10,000 employees or more	890	587,168	30,438,785	1,266,117,990	N/A

N/A - Receipts data are available for employers only for the years for which an economic census is taken (2002, 1997).

regulations has become one of the most significant business issues facing the life sciences industry today. IDC estimated that over 25 percent of the average IT budget of a pharmaceutical company is devoted to compliance issues.[13]

A significant regulation affecting these organizations is Part 11 of Title 21 U.S. Code of Federal Regulations (21 CFR 11). These requirements have a wide-ranging effect on how organizations store information electronically in databases and how they create records using word processors, spreadsheets, and graphics programs.

U.S. Public Sector

Public-sector agencies under the Department of Defense (DoD) generally look for guidance on security. The Defense Information Systems Agency (DISA, formerly known as the Defense Communications Agency) is a combat support agency of the United States DoD responsible for planning, developing, fielding, operating, and supporting command, control, communications, and information systems that serve the needs of the president, the secretary of defense, the joint chiefs of staff, and the combatant commanders under all conditions of peace and war.

DISA currently manages the Global Information Grid–Bandwidth Expansion (GIG-BE) program which reached Full Operational Capability (FOC) in 2005 and is now called the Defense Information Systems Network (DISN) Core.

DISA sets the standards and security regulations for the military SIPRnet (Secret [formerly Secure] Internet Protocol Router Network) and NIPRnet (Nonclassified Internet Protocol Router Network).

The CCA is a federal law that was coauthored by U.S. Representative William Clinger and Senator William Cohen in 1996. It is designed to improve the way the federal government acquires and manages IT. It requires the Department and individual programs to use performance-based management principles for acquiring IT. These principles include:

- Planning major IT investments
- Revising processes before investment
- Enforcing accountability for performance
- Using standards
- Increasing acquisition and incorporation of commercial technology
- Using modular contracting

In addition to CCA, the Foreign Intelligence Surveillance Act (FISA), and CFR, NARA regulations affect federal agencies and their records management programs.

Rules set by these regulations, and associated agencies, provide guidance, not only records management compliance, but often times on the technology used to store, safeguard, and manage content within a public agency. NARA rules span the life of public sector records and documents and can be found in Subchapter B of 36 Code of Federal Regulations Chapter XII. NARA has, in the past (NARA ERM Bulletin 2007-02) provided guidance ruling against the use of digital encryption technologies, including digital rights management (DRM) software. NARA is concerned that the application of encryption technologies, to digital Federal records, could impair the ability of the agencies to fulfill records management responsibilities under 36 CFR 1228.10. NARA has further expressed concern that, using Enterprise Records Management (ERM) programs, individual curators may set expiration dates that may conflict with authorized retention periods. This is not to say that NARA is opposed to ERM but rather is concerned about proper compliance with the rules regarding Federal Records.

Additional rules for ERM can be found in the Federal Information Processing Standards (FIPS) (Public Law 104-106). Under the authority of FIPS the Secretary of Commerce sets guidelines and implementation standards that are based on the National Institute of Standards and Technology (NIST) work. NIST develops standards for Federal government systems when there is a compelling requirement, such as a security or interoperability challenge that is not covered by an acceptable industry standard or solution.

"The Federal Information Security Management Act does not include a statutory provision allowing agencies to waive the provisions of mandatory Federal Information Processing Standards (FIPS). Waivers approved by the head of agencies had been allowed under the Computer Security Act, which was superseded by the Federal Information Security Management Act (FISMA). Therefore, the waiver procedures included in many FIPS are no longer in effect."[14] Essentially it is critical that agency leaders review and determine if the FIPS guidelines are mandatory for their agency. It is also good to note here that FIPS does not apply to national security systems (as defined in Title III, Information Security, of FISMA).

FROM THE REAL WORLD

Staying Compliant with Federal Information Processing Standards (FIPS)

"For many reasons, some applications may use cryptography that is not in compliance with U.S. Government Federal Information Processing Standards (FIPS) approved modes of operation. This reason may be compatibility with legacy systems. All applications that perform encryption or hashing can be compliant by using only the certified instances of the approved algorithms and by complying with the key generation and key management requirements either by using the Windows function for these or by complying to key generation and management requirements within the application. An implementation of a cryptographic algorithm is not considered FIPS 140 compliant if it has not been submitted for and passed NIST certification. This is true even if the implementation produces identical data as a certified implementation of the same algorithm. Be aware that locations may exist in an application where noncompliant algorithms or processes are allowed within a FIPS compliant application. For example, some internal processes that stay within the system or some external data that is to be additionally encrypted by a certified algorithm instance are allowed."

Many applications, such as Windows XP or Vista, have security settings that will allow you to set the local security or group policy to allow cryptographic algorithms that are FIPS 140 compliant and/or meet FIPS approved operating modes. Unfortunately these settings are only advisory in nature and do not constrain the other applications.

Source: Microsoft KnowledgeBase Article ID: 811833, Revision 2.1.

FROM THE REAL WORLD

Impact of Clinger–Cohen

The CCA generated a number of significant changes in the roles and responsibilities of various federal agencies in managing acquisition of IT. It elevated overall responsibility to the Director of the Office of Management and Budget (White House). The OMB set forth guidelines that must be followed by agencies.

At the agency level, IT management must be integrated into procurement, and procurement of commercial off-the-shelf technology was encouraged. CCA required each agency to name a chief information officer (CIO) with the responsibility for "developing, maintaining, and facilitating the implementation of a sound and integrated information technology architecture." The CIO is tasked with advising the agency director and senior staff on all IT issues.

Since these rules went into effect, the agency CIOs also have worked together to form the Federal CIO Council. Initially an informal group, the council's existence became codified into law by Congress in the [E-Government Act of 2002]. Official duties for the council include developing recommendations for government IT management policies, procedures, and standards; identifying opportunities to share information resources; and assessing and addressing the needs of the Federal Government's IT workforce.

In general, National Security Systems (NSS), as defined in the E-Government Act of 2002, are exempt from the act. However, there are specific exceptions to this exemption regarding: (1) capital planning and investment control (CPIC); (2) performance- and results-based management; agency CIO responsibilities; and (4) accountability.

In the DoD, the assistant secretary of defense for networks and information integration (or ASD [NII]) has been designated as the DoD CIO and provides management and oversight of all DoD information technology, including national security systems.[15]

Canada—Compliance Notes

The Canadian Competition Act (1993), when combined with the previous guidelines such as the Merger Enforcement Guidelines (1991), Misleading Advertising Guidelines (1991), the Predatory Pricing Enforcement Guidelines (1992), and the Price Discrimination Enforcement Guidelines (1992), provides many of the same stakeholder and broad economic safeguards outlined in legislation we have seen in the United States, Japan, and other countries around the globe.

The Competition Act underscores that though most firms comply with the law, all firms can benefit by implementing internal mechanisms to assist them in remaining in compliance with the current laws and regulations. Equally, as prevention mechanisms may not ensure perfect compliance, a corporate compliance program can also facilitate detection and remedial action by the firm in instances when anticompetitive conduct occurs. The Bulletin for the Competition Act

> . . . outlines the components of a credible and effective program. To be credible, a compliance program must demonstrate the company's commitment to conducting business in conformity with the act. To be effective, it needs to inform employees, officers and directors about the content of the act as it affects the company's business. It makes good business sense to implement an effective program that addresses both the criminal and civil reviewable provisions of the act. A good corporate compliance program can help to identify the boundaries of permissible conduct, as well as identify situations where it would be advisable to seek legal advice. A preemptive identification of areas of potential risk can save time and money, preserve goodwill, and set a company on a good track for the future. Knowing the limits of illegal conduct can free a company and its employees to pursue innovative and profitable business

practices. Many firms have already developed comprehensive compliance programs. Still others have instituted some or all of the highlighted elements on an informal or ad hoc basis and, for them, it may simply be a question of supplementing or formalizing what already exists. The decision to implement a compliance program is, of course, voluntary and the contents of a program are at the discretion of the firm implementing it. The goal of the Competition Bureau's work in the area of in-house compliance programs is to contribute to a business culture of respect for, and compliance with, the Competition Act.[16]

Australia—Compliance Notes

Similar to updates to legislation in the United States, the Commonwealth of Australia has recently updated corporate compliance programs. AS 3806 legislation seeks to provide a backbone of regulation for corporate governance. The 2006 version of AS 3806 contains many of the same provisions of the original standard written in 1998. The updated standard expands and adds additional compliance principles. Australian regulations call for the use of the standard by companies when establishing compliance frameworks.

Australia relies on the Australian Securities and Investment Commission (ASIC) and the Australian Prudential Regulation Authority (APRA) combined to oversee business compliance to the standard. The ASIC is an independent government body that acts as the regulator for Australian corporations. The ASIC's role is to enforce and regulate across the broad spectrum of companies to protect consumers, investors, and creditors. The APRA, however, is specifically focused on the regulation of the financial services industry.

Compliance regulators in Australia have most recently aimed their sharp eye at the pension industry. APRA has stiffened the bar for funds requiring stronger proof of adequate resources (human, technology and financial), risk management, and management skills to mitigate risks to stakeholders (employees, retirees, employers, and the public).

Compliance demands in the superannuation industry continue to increase due to the new licensing regime implemented by APRA. The new licensing regime requires trustees of superannuation funds to demonstrate to APRA that they have adequate resources (human, technology, and financial), risk management systems, and appropriate skills and expertise to manage the superannuation fund. The licensing regime has lifted the bar for superannuation trustees with a significant number of small to medium-size superannuation funds exiting the industry due to the increasing risk and compliance demands.

Australia Public Sector

The **Financial Management Standard 1997**[17] (also known as the **FMS**) is a state law of the Queensland Government empowered by the *Financial Administration and Audit Act 1977*[18] *(Qld)*. Its primary purpose is to provide the policies and principles to be observed in financial management, including planning, performance management, internal control, and corporate management within Queensland government.

This is achieved by stating the functions of each accountable officer and statutory body in relation to corporate management.

A key aspect of the FMS is its directives associated with management of Information and Communication Technology (ICT), including the requirement for detailed ICT planning to ensure appropriate acquisition processes and ongoing management.

Unlike the United States federal law known as the Information Technology Management Reform Act (also known as the Clinger-Cohen Act), the FMS contains explicit references to the use of Enterprise Architecture. In particular the FMS links the planning of ICT directly to the Government Enterprise Architecture.

Penalties, including imprisonment, exist for failure of accountable officers to comply with the requirements of the *Financial Administration and Audit Act 1977 (Qld)* and associated regulations and the FMS.

United Kingdom—Compliance Notes

Business compliance in the United Kingdom, as with all countries associated with the European Union (EU), is a matter of layered laws and regulations. As in other countries, there is a series of alphabet agencies that provide policies and regulation including the Financial Services Authority (FSA), the Environment Protection Agency (EPA), and the Information Commissioner.

The FSA Register provides an online search for firms that are or have been regulated by the FSA under the Financial Services & Markets Act 2000 (FSMA), which came into force on December 1, 2001.

The FSA not only provides a framework for financial institution governance but can be called upon by the government in times of crisis in the financial industry to attempt to divert disaster. One recent example is the case of Northern Rock's high-risk investment failures in hedge funds. When all other alternative funding schemes appear to fail, the Chancellor, Alistair Darling, told the *Financial Times* (January 21, 2008) he is planning to give the FSA more power to deal with failing banks to avoid another Northern Rock–style crisis. He proposes giving the FSA the power to seize and protect customers' cash if their bank gets into difficulties.[19]

Overseeing compliance for all organizations that process or hold personal data are the Data Protection Act (DPA[20]) and the Freedom of Information Act of 2000. Under the DPA, as in most countries in the EU, the protection of personal data are defined as follows:

- Data which relates to a living individual who can be identified;
- From those data; or
- From those data and other information which is in the possession of, or is likely to come into the possession of, the data controller and includes any expression of opinion about the individual and any indication of the intentions of the data controller or any other person in respect of the individual.[21]

FROM THE REAL WORLD

U.K. Data Protection Act

The U.K. Data Protection Act (DPA) is a complex body of law. There are eight common sense rules known as the Data Protection Principles that require personal information to be:

❶ Fairly and lawfully processed
❷ Processed for limited purposes

❸ Adequate, relevant, and not excessive in relations to the purpose they were collected

❹ Accurate

❺ Not kept longer than necessary

❻ Processed in accordance with the rights of the data subjects (under the Act)

❼ Kept secure

❽ Not transferred abroad without adequate protection

In addition, "the act provides stronger protection for sensitive information about your ethnic origins, political opinions, religious beliefs, trade union membership, health, sexual life, and any marital history."

The Office of Information Commissioner (an independent government authority) is responsible for compliance and guidance regarding the act. The complexity of the act can also enable organizations to hide behind the act and not even provide very basic public access to data.[22]

REMEDY

Sections 55 and 56 regards the unlawful obtaining of personal data a criminal offense. This section of the act addresses the acquisition by individuals, such as hackers or identify thieves, who would obtain personal data without permission.

Complications with the Criminal Records Bureau providing a basic disclosure service has resulted in limited or no use of the criminal sanctions against individuals (as of 2007).

Where the DPA sought to protect personal data, essentially governing the behavior of business, the Freedom of Information Act of 2000 provides access to data held by public agencies in the United Kingdom.[23]

Japan—Compliance Notes

FROM THE REAL WORLD

Japan Fair Trade Commission

"The JFTC has made clear that it will not file a criminal accusation against the first enterprise that files an application before the initiation of an investigation as well as officers and employees of the applicants."

In 2007, Kazuhiko Takeshima cited the importance of the JFTC "to play a significant role as the competition authority in order to ensure sound and effective competition."

Source: Kazuhiko Takeshima, Chairman JFTC, "Endeavour to Establish a Rigorous Enforcement of the Antimonopoly Act in Japan," May 3, 2007.

In Japan, on October 7, 2005, the Fair Trade Commission (JFTC) amended the Act Concerning the Prohibition of Private Monopolization and Maintenance of Fair Trade (Act No. 35 of 2005). The JFTC introduced provisions requiring compulsory investigation of cases concerning offenses (stipulated in Section 89 through 91 of the Act Concerning the Prohibition of Private Monopolization and Maintenance of Fair Trade). In order to ensure appropriate enforcement of the amended act, the JFTC will investigate and file a criminal accusation based on violations of the amended act.

The Policy on Criminal Accusation

1. The JFTC will actively accuse to seek criminal penalties on the following cases:

(a) Vicious and serious cases which are considered to have widespread influence on people's livings, out of those violations which substantially restrain competition in certain areas of trade such as price-fixing cartels, supply-restraint cartels, market allocations, bid-rigging, group boycotts, and other violations.

(b) Among violation cases involving those firms or industries who are repeat offenders or those who do not abide by the elimination measures, those cases for which the administrative measures of the JFTC are not considered to fulfill the purpose of the act.

2. However, the JFTC will not file accusations against the following persons:

(a) The first entrepreneur that submitted reports and materials concerning the immunity from the surcharge before the investigation start date. (The entrepreneur that submits reports and materials pursuant to the provision of Section 7-2 (7) of the act.) However, this provision shall not apply to the entrepreneur who's behavior falls under any of the paragraphs of Section 7-2 (12) of the act; the said reports or documents contain false information, the said entrepreneur fails to submit the reports or materials or submits false reports or materials in response to the additional requests, and the said entrepreneur coerced another entrepreneur to commit the volatile act or blocked another entrepreneur from ceasing to commit the volatile act.

(b) The officer, employee, or other person of the said entrepreneur who committed the volatile act of the act and
is deemed to be in a circumstance to be treated as same
as the said entrepreneur, regarding the said entrepreneur's submission of reports and materials to the JFTC,
response to the investigation by the JFTC following the
said submission, and others.

Germany—Compliance Notes

The Code of Best Practice for Germany was adopted on February
26, 2002. The main point of the Code was to improve corporate
governance practices relating to managing, directing, and overseeing publicly registered corporations. The code is specific to publicly
listed companies but is not mandatory. If publicly listed companies
do not comply, they must "explain" their noncompliance. Though
compliance is not mandatory, the Code was introduced through a
statutory provision (section 161 of the Aktiengesetz [AktG]). This
approach levies a statutory duty on the boards and management
of listed corporations to comply or explain noncompliance on an
annual basis. The compliance/noncompliance declaration must be
made available to the shareholders annually and available at all times.

As in the United Kingdom, Germany has instituted a personal
data protection act, the Bundesdatenschutzgesetz (BDSG, German
Federal Data Protection Act). "The BDSG only applies to information
concerning the personal or material circumstances of an identified or
identifiable individual (personal data). The act does not cover information relating to companies or other legally established entities."[24]

Daimler Chrysler

Corporate Governance issues are, quite rightly, receiving ever more attention and are being discussed by the general public.

Daimler supports the various initiatives which are intended to improve Corporate Governance. Our company has been practicing many of the principles arising from these initiatives for a long time.

As a globally oriented company we are particularly interested in aligning the Daimler Corporate Governance system internationally and making it transparent. The information given here aims to enhance this transparency.

Source: www.daimlerchrysler.com/corpgov_e.

Mexico or Other Latin American Country—Compliance Notes

Mexico, under the leadership of President Fox, in 2001 enacted a new capital markets law that improved the corporate governance standards of Mexican public companies. This law brought Mexican efforts in line with others in Latin America, including the Chilean public share offering (OPA) law, aimed at managing tender offers, and the Brazilian Corporate Law reform. As a group, these laws are aimed at bringing corporate governance in Latin American in line with similar legislation around the world.

Chapter Summary

To restate the basic premise: Governance policy is essentially designed and monitored by the board of directors or agency leadership to promote the interests of the stakeholders (owners or citizens). Governance policy is guided by the prevailing laws within the countries the enterprise operates, balancing the objectives, goals, and, often, the beliefs of the stakeholders. This policy is then translated into compliance rules, procedures, and systems by management.

Though governance and compliance structures are often more reflective of the enterprise maturity, all enterprise governance is guided by the external regulations of both the home and foreign operating environments.

In the United States, the most broadly quoted legislation, the Sarbanes-Oxley Act (2002) and the U.S. Foreign Corrupt Practices Act, require reporting companies to keep books and records with reasonable detail to accurately reflect transactions. These acts, as well as most of the non-U.S. acts discussed in this chapter, require companies to maintain a system of internal accounting controls, sufficient to provide reasonable assurance to stakeholders that transactions were properly executed and governance standards maintained.

If governance is about guidance, compliance is about execution. Compliance refers to the procedures, systems, or organizations at corporations and public agencies created to ensure that personnel are aware of and take steps to comply with not only relevant laws and regulations but also the specific rules of governance provided by the enterprise leadership.

The relationship between governance, formed by a representative of the stakeholders (e.g., a board of directors or elected leadership), and compliance, executed by managers, should be clear but is often a confusing maze run by various levels of supervision and employees.

Strengthening and improving organizational governance and compliance is a concern of most, regardless of location. It is important to keep in mind the local nature of law when viewing governance and compliance. Changes in legislation within the United States, though often influencing others, has no impact on the legal operation of an enterprise in the United Kingdom or Japan. The governments, business leaders, and investors around the world influence one another through the dynamics of the global economy. By law, U.S. companies operating anywhere in the world are still bound by U.S. law, as well as the laws of the other countries in which they choose to operate. Conversely, a Korean company operating in the United States is bound by Korean law first, while its U.S. operations are bound by U.S. law first.

As we look across the legal framework evolving around the world, we see similarities of intent and structure. Strong themes emerging around the world are responsibility, transparency, and compliance. Throughout our discussion, we will look not only at the context of these drivers but also at how they can become part of the enterprise culture and workflow.

Notes

1. Art Durnev and E. Han Kim, "To Steal or Not to Steal: Firm Attributes, Legal Environment, and Valuation" 14th Annual Conference on Financial Economics and Accounting (FEA), September 22, 2003; AFA 2004 San Diego Meetings. Available at SSRN: http://ssrn.com/abstract=391132 or DOI: 10.2139/ssrn.391132.

2. Carolyn Kay Brancato and Christian A. Plath, "Corporate Governance Handbook 2005: Developments in Best Practices, Compliance, and Legal Standards," Special Report 05-02.

3. Ibid.

4. The Information Technology Management Reform Act of 1996 and the Federal Acquisition Reform Act (FARA) of 1996 were combined to become the Clinger-Cohen Act of 1996 (CCA). The CCA repealed the earlier Brooks Automatic Data Processing Act, so that agencies did not have to obtain information technology procurement authority from the General Services Administration.

5. www.ussc.gov/2007guid/8b2_1.html.

6. U.S. Small Business Administration, "Statistics about Business Size (Including Small Business) from the U.S. Census Bureau," www.census.gov/epcd/www/smallbus.html.

7. www.business.gov.

8. The Gramm-Leach-Bliley Act, also known as the GLBA Financial Services Modernization Act, Pub. L. No 106-102, 113 Stat. 1338 (Nov 12 1999). Passed by the U.S. Congress, it repealed the Glass-Steagall Act and allowed for competition among banks, securities companies, and insurance companies (which had been expressly forbidden by the Glass-Steagall Act). The GLBA allowed the merger of commercial and investment banking (e.g., Citibank [bank] with Travelers Group [insurance] forming Citigroup). GLBA essentially created what is commonly called the financial services industry today in the United States.

9. FISMA (44 USC, Section 3541, et seq.) is Title III of the E-Government Act of 2002 (Pub L. 107-347, 116 Stat 2899).

This Act is intended to strengthen the computer and network security within the Federal Government and its partners (government contractors). Essentially, FISMA mandates yearly audits. The audits have underscored serious challenges in e-security with the average score of 64% in 2003 and 67.3% in 2004 (www.compliancehome.com/resources/FISMA/Regulations/abstract10213.html). A deeper discussion of this topic can be found in Part II of this book.

10. HIPAA (1996) provides in Title I health insurance coverage for workers and their families when they change or lose their jobs. Title II of HIPAA, the Administrative Supplication (AS) provisions, provides requirements for the national standards for electronic health care transactions and national identifiers for health care providers, health insurance plans, and employers. Additionally, Title II provides regulations regarding security and privacy of health data. The implied intent is to support the streamlining of the nation's health care system and promote the use of electronic data interchange (EDI) in the U.S. health care system. A deeper discussion of the topic can be found in Part II of this book.

11. COBIT is a set of guidelines, framework, for information technology (IT) management established by the Information Systems Audit and Control Association (ISACA), and the IT Governance Institute (ITGI) in 1992. COBIT gives broad guidance to managers, auditors, and IT users with a set of generally accepted measures, indicators, processes, and best practices to assist them in maximizing the benefits derived through the use of IT and developing appropriate IT governance and controls.

12. NIST is the federal technology agency that works with industry to develop and apply technology, measurements, and standards.

13. IDC/Revenue Recognition.com Financial executive benchmarking panel survey – SOX edition 2005.

14. Federal Information Processing Standards Publications (FIPS PUBS), www.itl.nist.gov/fipspubs/.

15. House Government Reform Committee's Subcommittee on Technology, Information Policy, Intergovernmental Relations, and the Census, December 9th, 2003.

16. Konrad von Finckenstein, Q.C., Director of Investigation and Research, *Competition Act,* Corporate Compliance Programs, June 1997.

17. Purpose of FMS: The primary purpose of this standard is to provide for the following:

    1. Requirements for annual financial statements of departments, and

    2. Prescribed accounting standards for a financial year ending before July 1, 2005:

    (a) the policies and principles to be observed in financial management, including planning, performance management, internal control, and corporate management;

    (b) the content of financial statements, final financial statements, annual reports, and final reports;

    (c) the matters to be included in manuals.

The secondary purpose is achieved by stating the functions of each accountable officer, former accountable officer, statutory body, and administering department about matters for which this standard may be made.

18. Financial Administration and Audit Act 1977: An Act to provide for the financial administration and audit of the State's public finances, of departments and statutory bodies, for the audit of associated bodies and for other matters.

19. BBC News, Timeline: Northern Rock bank crisis, January 21, 2008, http://news.bbc.co.uk/1/hi/business/7007076.stm.

20. DPA provides a legal basis for the privacy and protection of personal data in the United Kingdom. The Act places restrictions on the collection or holding of data which can identify a living person. The Act does not apply to domestic use, for example keeping a personal address book.

21. www.dataprotectionact.org/2.html.

22. www.legislation.org.uk/intro.htm.

23. www.opsi.gov.uk/acts/acts2000/ukpga_20000036_en_1.

24. Jutta Geiger, The Transfer of Data Abroad by Private Sector Companies: Data Protection Under the German Federal Data Protection Act, *German Law Journal* No 4, August 1, 2003.

Framework for Governance

Part II will attempt to answer some major questions regarding the role that technology should play in managing compliance. Can technology help to address the growing regulatory overhead, reducing the complexity and improving productivity? How do organizations manage and record decisions and actions made by existing or potential employees and directors? How are these processes related to compliance and governance? How technology is used can have a large impact on the effectiveness of any enterprise compliance program, for better or for worse!

CHAPTER 3

A Framework for Governance

After reading this chapter, you will be able to:

- Describe a well-articulated compliance framework.
- Articulate actions that will enable and support compliance within the enterprise.
- Understand the concept of integrating compliance into the "way we work."
- Review the guidelines for compliance models.
- Weigh the benefits of different models.

Introduction

It is difficult enough to meet local requirements, but when your workforce is scattered across the globe, the challenge can be overwhelming. As the work environment goes global, it can become a serious part of the information manager's job to ensure compliance across a global network. To minimize the impact on productivity, information-centric workers (I-workers) require compliance-related tasks built into their day-to-day business processes, allowing them to utilize the applications they already use on a daily basis to ensure that they are compliant. Working locally but thinking globally is a reality today.

Recalling our earlier discussion on the risk-compliance-mitigation relationship, the greatest and most difficult risk to mitigate is ignorance (see Exhibit 3.1)—not of the work to be accomplished but

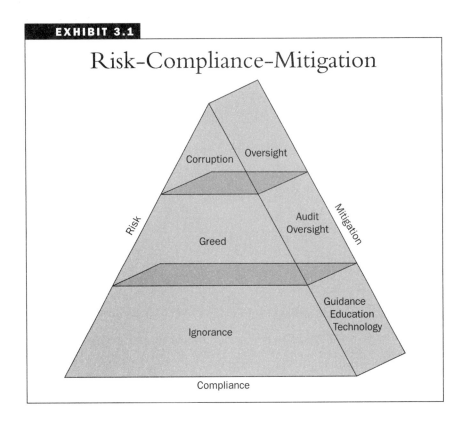

EXHIBIT 3.1

Risk-Compliance-Mitigation

Corruption Oversight

Risk

Audit Oversight

Mitigation

Greed

Guidance Education Technology

Ignorance

Compliance

ignorance of an ever-increasing set of business rules that ensure compliance and security.

Being good at your job requires subject-matter expertise as well as knowledge of required compliance rules and procedures. Given the broad number of rules, especially in global work environments, on-the-job education is often insufficient to ensure compliance. If errors are encountered, it is also critical that good tracking and audit trails are available to mitigate the impact of violations.

Compliance goes beyond simply containing information. Compliance policies today extend into the management of intellectual property (IP) rights, authorization, and security considerations. U.S. Sarbanes-Oxley (SOX) 404 rules, and similar rules around the world, call for information transparency clearly dictating that the board of directors, management, and stakeholders must have clear vision into the operation of the business.

Throughout this section we will focus on some of the techniques available today to support the distribution of guidance and education as well as data transparency through workflow management and technology support.

Do As I Say—Providing Continuous Guidance

Throughout this discussion, we will talk about new ways to embed guidance in the *way we work*. Ever consider giving up compliance training? Well, let's not go that far, but it is time to open our minds—and work environments—to new ideas on compliance guidance. The potential for continuous guidance is emerging today through the use of workflow managers, collaborative workspaces,

EXHIBIT 3.2

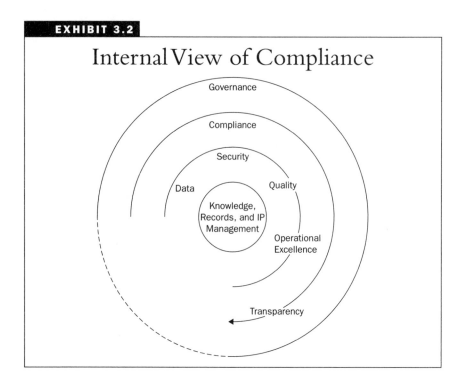

Internal View of Compliance

and even desktop software.[1] New ways to guide employee operations as well as track regulatory compliance from within the existing desktop (or desktop application) environment are now a reality. The use of these techniques must be carefully thought out and implemented within the confines of the well-designed structure enabled by technology.

When we began this discussion we talked about the centrality of governance as the guiding light or foundation for enterprise compliance. As shown in Exhibit 3.2, from an internal perspective, the governance and compliance framework seeks to secure, through the strict management of data flow, the information (knowledge and IP) of the enterprise.

Business Rules and Structure Are the Foundation of an Enterprise

The rules and organizational structures outline the controls, processes mechanisms, and standard operating procedures (SOPs) that need to be followed and possibly adapted by managers when incorporating compliance requirements. Auditor recommendations and the compliance strategy are the foundation on which an enterprise builds its rules and structures.

New compliance activities are generally expressed at a low level of granularity and often take considerable resources and time to understand, validate, document, and enforce. However, these controls, processes, and standards are the foundation for the compliance program and cannot be underestimated or ignored because they take time to implement. Instead, perceptive executives are calling for solutions to be engineered prior to implementing a technology solution to accelerate the delivery and milestone deliverables. The information generated by these controls and processes needs to be reported for compliance and leveraged to provide greater benefit and to validate the implantation of governance.

Step 1: Governance Policy

To ensure a sustainable compliance approach, a strong governance model is required. As we stated in Chapter 1, the governance framework does not have to be visible to most of the user community, but it is the core guidance for the compliance program and policies that will be reviewed by the auditors. The governance policy should bring clarity and unify the multitude of messages and initiatives within the enterprise to gain efficiency and to reduce compliance risks. Often, there are similar information management initiatives within the organization that can be condensed to gain immediate benefits, for example, internal news activities, team sharing processes, and country-specific compliance teams.

Step 2: Fostering a Compliance Culture

Traditional records management and compliance programs have focused on compliance officer roles and specific business processes. These programs have also traditionally focused on providing tactical technology solutions. A tactical or silo-based approach often results in the utmost frustration for management and users due to the constant changes of technologies and day-to-day tasks.

The new, competitive advantage era of compliance programs requires the programs to deliver sustainable benefits; this can be achieved only through analysis and change. Fostering a culture of compliance is essential to success and is a constant activity during previous and future pillars.

To help ensure that the user community accepts the new ways of working and can see real benefits, the significant culture change must be addressed. If the users do not accept all of the new, end-to-end processes, policies, controls, and technologies, the program will have a higher chance of failure, and the organization will be more prone to missing its compliance requirements.

Step 3: Managing the Information Flow

Information management (IM)—both the technology and information it carries—is perhaps the most complex and rapidly changing area, due to accelerating technology advancements such as instant messaging, personal digital assistants (PDAs), and so on. This pillar ties together the enabler (technology) and the business (governance, culture, and process) using IM and enterprise content management (ECM). It looks at how the requirements of the business affect the users and their day-to-day life. In addition, it ensures that all the information is controlled and processed in a manner that meets the auditors' requirements.

A compliance framework must include the policies, procedures, controls, guidance, and training for the entire life cycle of all information in the organization. IM solutions, internally established to meet rules such as SOX or guidance from agencies such as the National Archives and Records Agency (NARA) for public-sector enterprises, must provide and govern the activities required to ensure that information is correctly created, maintained, reviewed, and disposed of. These activities are critical to demonstrate accountability and traceability for auditing. The technology and records management solution must also ensure that the user is provided with an easy-to-use technical environment, and it must support the tasks the user needs to perform.

A risk management approach is now a common element of the IM policies and guidelines for the majority of organizations. The key element in IM risk management is a controls-based approach. The resulting solution is often based on industry-specific standards such as Control Objectives for Information and Related Technology (COBIT—the basis for the Financial Services industry approach and key to the European Markets in Financial Instruments Directive [MiFID] legislation).

Building a Compliance Model

The U.S. Securities and Exchange Commission (SEC) rules require companies to identify the evolution framework used by management to assess the effectiveness of the company's internal controls and reporting. The rule does not demand a specific framework. It does require, though, a recognizable structure that:

- Is bias free.

- Assures consistent qualitative and quantitative measurement of internal control.

- Presents a complete picture, including those relevant factors that might affect the effectiveness of a company's internal controls.

- Provides guidance for an evaluation of internal control.

Regulatory obligations, such as SOX or Basel II, are increasing demand for automated control monitoring solutions, which can help reduce the cost and disruption that compliance often brings to large organizations. The SEC has been working closely with the Public Company Accounting Oversight Board[2] (PCAOB) to provide direction in order to help companies reduce excessive testing of controls and related costs. In June 2007, the SEC published interpretive guidance regarding SOX compliance and in the prior month the PCAOB released a new U.S. Auditing Standard[3] (AS 5) based on a top-down approach. While guidance from the SEC is somewhat general, the new PCAOB auditing standard is very specific and based on four primary principles:

1. *Focus the audit on the most important matters.* Implement a top-down, risk-based approach where energy is devoted proportionately to areas with the most-to-least impact on financial reporting.

2. *Eliminate unnecessary procedures.* Make use of audit knowledge from previous years, particularly noting deficiencies identified in the prior year, in addition to making use of recent internal audit work. The auditor may also use a *benchmarking* strategy for automated application controls to reduce testing in subsequent years.

3. *Scale the audit for smaller companies.* External auditors are encouraged to scale the audit based on the size and complexity of the company, rather than taking a one-size-fits-all approach.

4. *Simplify the requirements.* The level of detail and specificity has been reduced to encourage auditors to apply professional judgment under the facts and circumstances.

Optimized Compliance Management (OCM)

OCM is the alignment of an organization's governance and compliance requirements to its strategic goals. To support an initial implementation of and subsequent improvements to OCM, a standard structure called the *optimized compliance framework (OCF)*, outlined in Exhibit 3.3, is recommended for adoption by an enterprise. Specifically, this framework should define a methodology, customized for the organization, for implementing and improving OCM. Such a framework, as outlined earlier, is an iterative cycle that emphasizes assessment and continuous improvement. In the broadest sense, an OCF is a maturity model.

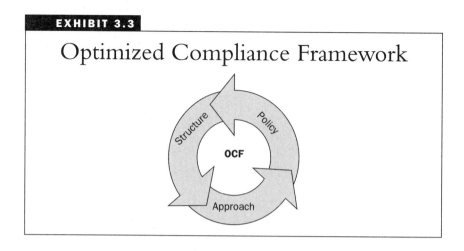

EXHIBIT 3.3

Optimized Compliance Framework

However, it is different from many other maturity models (such as the Capabilities Maturity Model [CMM]) in that it defines a continuum of maturity as opposed to discrete maturity levels.

	Functions	Guidance
1	Governance Policy	Laws and regulations (discussed in Part I)
2	Compliance Structure	Industry-recognized best practices (discussed in Part II)
3	Workforce Mitigation Approach	Level of implementation of current practices (discussed in Part II)

The fact that the OCF is presented as a continuous improvement cycle implies the need for review and improvement of the framework components on a routine basis. Successful development of an OCF requires explicit buy-in by senior management, as they determine strategy, and must provide insights into the objectives of the organization. Further, overall success potential is increased by taking advantage of the iterative nature of the framework (for associated business units) to take advantage of the "low-hanging fruit" in the initial stages to build confidence in the process.

OCM can benefit organizations by ensuring effective implementation of requirements while maintaining operating efficiency. An organization-wide OCM standard provides a cost savings that is associated with the elimination of random programs that are not tied to the organization's strategic goals. It can also enhance the prestige of the compliance efforts in the organization by positioning it as a critical partner in strategic planning instead of administrative overhead cost.

Though most of the legislation and regulations regarding governance and compliance are focused on financial transactions, some, like the U.S. Foreign Corrupt Practices Act also seek to assure proper management of assets by preventing unauthorized transactions and internal accounting controls, designed to provide reasonable assurance that the organization's transactions are properly managed and assets are safeguarded. Most parties interpret this to mean that *generally accepted accounting principles* (GAAP) are followed. Defining an acceptable framework for the execution of governance policy is not a new or novel concept. In 1992, in the United States, the Committee of Sponsoring Organizations (COSO) was formed from the work of the Treadway Commission (National Commission on Fraudulent Financial Reporting), which published a report on internal controls as guidance to managers, boards, and auditors.

Effectiveness of controls must be assessed for all areas of the compliance framework (Control Activities, Control Environment, Risk Assessment, Monitoring, Information, and Communications) not just the Control Activities. Compliance monitoring is an iterative process

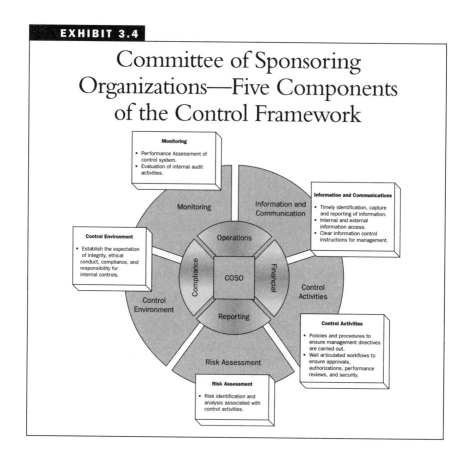

EXHIBIT 3.4

Committee of Sponsoring Organizations—Five Components of the Control Framework

and requires proactive operational action plans that guide the organization in the challenging process of supporting the quarterly and annual controls certifications.

Briefly walking through the five actions described in Exhibit 3.4 at a high level, we note that:

- Monitoring is a proactive assessment of the control system over time.
- Information and Communications calls for access and flow of information at all levels of the enterprise.

- Control Activities establishes policies and procedures that ensure directives are carried out at all levels.
- Risk Assessment is the identification and analysis of risk related to achieving compliance objectives.
- Control Environment sets the tone, influencing control consciousness.

As organizations mature, they go through phases much as people do. When they are young, they are brash and often take foolish risks. As they grow older, they learn what behaviors produce positive results and what behaviors result in negative outcomes. Establishing sound governance guidelines is the initial step quickly followed by compliance framework. A framework simply provides an outline for execution. In the following chapter we will explore, at the ground level, new and innovative ways your organization can start to deliver on the compliance framework while maintaining a high standard for service/product delivery.

Chapter Summary

Compliance is no longer an add-on to the business but an essential part of business *as usual,* ideally totally embedded across all areas, activities, and regions. These new practices need to provide sustainable business value across multiple areas of the business, for example, culture, information management, governance, business processes, and an enabling technology platform.

Notes

1. Office Business Application (OBA) capabilities, meaning that users can perform compliance activities such as monitoring,

analysis, and auditing from within familiar applications like SharePoint Server, Outlook, Excel, and InfoPath.

2. The SOX Act created the PCAOB, an organization whose purpose is to oversee the auditors of public companies in order to protect the interests of investors. The PCAOB operates under the SEC.

3. AS 5 supersedes AS 2 and is the auditing standard on attestation engagements referred to by Section 404(b) of the SOX.

CHAPTER 4

Exploring the Potential

After reading this chapter, you will be able to:

- Review how a compliance framework can enhance enterprise compliance.
- Evaluate the benefits of controls.
- Understand how technology is a critical component of an effective compliance effort.

Few business issues are higher profile than compliance. As we have noted, the number and scope of compliance regulations have increased dramatically over the last few years, making compliance an increasingly complex business and technology challenge. Whether aimed to prevent fraud and money laundering, to combat international terrorism, or to ensure financial accountability and privacy, a kaleidoscope of international, federal, and state regulations—such as the USA PATRIOT Act, Sarbanes-Oxley (SOX), Basel II, Bank of England, Bank Secrecy Act, Health Insurance Portability and Accountability Act (HIPAA), and others—dramatically impacts how companies do business.

To be successful, organizations that are serious about compliance must also be serious about data quality because at the core of any reliable compliance program is quality data. Ideally, an organization's compliance software will provide specialized data quality and matching capabilities as part of an all-encompassing enterprise compliance and case-management solution.

Organizations that have pieced together their compliance process should carefully review its design and audit its results to ensure that the process that has developed over time is up to the task of meeting the company's current requirements. In particular, organizations that plan to use existing data quality software for their compliance efforts must carefully examine the software's ability to effectively extend its rules and processing capabilities in order to provide mission-critical and compliance-specific capabilities, without which the entire compliance process could be undermined.

Today's C-level executives manage in a global economy while struggling with local (federal or state) regulation. Given the tangible and intangible cost of alleged ethical conflict, such as harm to reputation, investigation expense, and lower stakeholder morale, organizations today are pressed to develop more reliable methods of tracking and recording compliance-related actions of employees and directors. In this global economy, tracing and recording work activities is being taken to a new level of complexity and interdependence. Where once it was enough to perform linear tasks, it is now necessary to drive strategy and compliance as well as daily processing tasks. This book discusses some of the issues related to corporate compliance, governance, and ethics as well as methods of tracking and recording employee- and director-related activities.

Driving Influence: How Can Organizations Establish or Foster a Culture of Compliance that Fosters Transparency and Objectivity?

There are three well-used approaches to these challenges:

1. Employees and directors are expected to proactively reference the compliance policies and procedures within their organizations or consult with their supervisors, compliance officer, or compliance service provider (attorney) about any potential transaction that may lead to a conflict or violation.

2. Employees and directors complete and sign forms that contain transactional information such as expense, entertainment, outside interests, gifts, and trading accounts that are signed and then reviewed to make certain that the transactions are kept within the rules defined by policy and procedures.

3. Employees and directors complete a questionnaire that requires declarative statements about their past activities.

Looking at New Practices

SOX, Basel II, and other compliance legislation will always require additional investment though there are ways to reduce the time and cost of implementation. For example, with recent guidance from the Securities and Exchange Commission (SEC) and new auditing standard (AS 5) for SOX, the availability of automated technology, compliance efforts can actually lead to improved productivity and overall cost reductions. The use of automated software tools is a vital component of any strategy designed to achieve sustainable compliance. Technology cannot solve a challenge that does not have clear definition. Throughout our discussion we have stressed the importance of customizing the generic models for use within your unique enterprise, including:

- Creating a (three-step) governance/compliance policy.
- Customizing a generic compliance framework (such as COSO) into an enterprise optimized compliance framework (OCF).
- Using a simplified auditing standard (such as AS 5).

To achieve compliance, improve productivity, and generally optimize enterprise work, it is necessary to establish a set of technology guidelines as well. Technology enablement for information-centric work calls for three basic components: rules, management, and tracking.

1. *Managing by rules.* Codifying procedural rules to streamline pathways to outcomes resulting in legal, ethical, and enterprise advice (such as under the conditions selected this transaction can proceed) or hand-offs (such as please consult with your compliance officer). The streamlining methodology focuses on the optimal steps to reach an outcome. The codification of the rules is a unique combination recommended in this book of legal, human resources, and business analysis.

This is followed by quality structure walkthroughs to ensure that the combined approach is compatible with the business under study.

2. *Managing workflow.* Use of bundling procedures into technology-enabled workflows (such as intranet web components or Microsoft SharePoint Workflow manager) enforces consistency from any point (such as online forms, service help desk). The complexities of the procedures are masked so that compliance is assured regardless of the path the employee or director takes in executing the activity.

3. *Managing metrics.* All workflow activities can be tracked and recorded if they are connected to an underlying database. Based on the rules associated with the procedure, all or some of the activity-related data as well as the tasks themselves can be recorded, such as identity of the user, date, durations, and so on, increasing transparency and timeline auditing. Metrics of this type can be automatically generated from the workflow and desktop application concepts outlined in Part II of this book.

Technologies Can Help Achieve the Vision

Technology is the enabler of business rules, governance, culture, and information management. The enabling information technology (IT) platform should provide an enterprise-wide solution to meet these requirements. The platform should be designed in a manner that is scalable, secure, integrateable, and, above all, intuitive to the user community.

Over the past few years, multiple niche solutions have come to market that provide a solution specific to one legislation or regulation. Demand has also risen for enterprise-level solutions that provide content, compliance, workflow, search, and document composition features.

A compliance plan should allow for changing legislation and regulations in a sensible, cost-effective, and future-proof manner. The plan should present a familiar and easy-to-use interface, a control-based workflow, enterprise content management (ECM), and a secure architecture.

Most office environments rarely have only one application on their desktop or only one supplier of line-of-business (LOB) applications, so a scalable compliance solution must address many applications and modes of work and provide updated information to the user as quickly as possible. The solution must address both the *people* requirements and *business* needs through strong *application* functionality, tight *integration*, leveraged *data* repositories, and a security-enhanced *infrastructure*.

Today, integrated desktop technology environments can be used to meet compliance and collaborative requirements ranging from the demands of the infrastructure to those of the people in a cost-effective manner. Users interact with enterprise solutions through the familiar desktop environments, such as Microsoft Office or Lotus Notes, web browsers, and even LOB applications. These platforms can provide one view of all information from multiple sources, reducing the learning curve and allowing for tracking while providing guidance in workflow support.

To help ensure that the solution platform is robust, compliant, and as secure as possible, many vendors have put forward technology solutions that meet some or all of the conditions outlined above. When evaluating these solutions, it is best to create a checklist (as provided in Appendix B from Microsoft Corporation) to ensure that the solution will help to identify specific control objectives (such as document tracking for legal discovery) from key legislation (such as SOX) and regulations (such as those listed by Basel II) for an organization's IT department. These control objectives provide a basis from which to implement controls and manage the regulatory compliance process for your organization. The framework provides a means to map technology solutions to each control objective and, in turn, to the regulations/legislations.

In the following chapter, we will look at some key compliance areas required by most enterprises and the technology ideas that are commonly available today to support them. Our goal is to take our discussion from the theoretical to the practical.

Supporting Regulation through Technology Enablement

Over the past decade, technology vendors have rushed to create compliance support components to their existing and new programs. This support is most evident at the desktop around the legal discovery process and records management processes/policies. Product literature now tells us that features of these products will enhance an enterprise's efforts to meet country-specific legislation such as SOX and 21 Code of Federal Regulations (CFR) Part 11. Vendors and consultants have spent millions to adapt features and map them to the latest thinking in compliance programs focused on aligning organizational culture, information management, process, governance, and IT platform to help create "out-of-the-box" compliance.

FROM THE REAL WORLD

How Del Monte Foods Used Technology to Leverage ECM and Compliance to Develop Market Share

The Company

Del Monte Foods is a U.S. distributor of canned fruits, vegetables, and tomatoes, with over 3,400 products.

The Challenge

Del Monte sought to drive innovation, streamline the product development process, and comply with regulatory requirement such as SOX.

The Solution and Benefits

Through the integration of collaborative tools including automated processes and built-in workflows for handling asset requests and approvals, Del Monte Foods improved delivery efficiency and effectiveness. Previously, Del Monte's IT department found itself wanting to increase its efficiency in preparing for various Sarbanes-Oxley audits. Now, with an effective tracking system and a consolidated data repository, IT staff no longer spends as much time on manually locating e-mails or documents to meet compliance requirements. Process standardization and automation resulted in both time savings and enhanced security with enhanced visibility into the process. They:

- Enable information-sharing document collaboration.
- Improve regulatory compliance requirements.

This enables the company to:

- Improve the time to market.
- Reduce the cost of managing (hours invested) product development data and compliance.
- Create better-quality products.
- Improve compliance and product defect responsiveness to differentiate Del Monte from its competitors.[1]

Many of these solutions provide processes, controls, and policies for compliance activities that are applicable across all industries and regulations. In the following pages we will discuss how your enterprise might consider using technology to meet key regulations. Understanding the benefits of "out-of-the-box" solutions is important when considering purchasing and/or upgrading capabilities to improve compliance. Technology solutions are typically introduced as part of a strategic plan and, due to the cost of implementation, should address multiple compliance drivers. In the following discussion, we will discuss two specific regulations to show how technology solutions can align to compliance goals.

Regulatory legislation discussed in Chapter 1, such as SOX or Basel II, require technologies for functions such as large transaction-based auditing. By providing technologies for auditing and workflow, organizations can enhance their existing processes for controlling and reporting information in a long-term, strategic manner. Integrated, security-enhanced, and centrally managed workspaces, provided by a number of vendors today, reduce exposure of confidential information, helping ensure compliance throughout workflow processes.

SOX, as we discussed earlier, places considerable pressure from the SEC as well as the public (media and stockholders) on compliance. The consequences of noncompliance are designed to be considerable and make executives consider the cost of compliance well worth the investment. Upgrading existing desktop tools that contain compliance-enabling features can help to mitigate the cost of compliance programs. New program features provide embedded controls and managed process workflows. Integrated workflows that enforce policies, controls, and correct procedure can provide more than the means for becoming compliant—they can provide tangible benefits as well.

By adopting strong accounting and control practices, organizations can reduce exposure to documentation inefficiencies and financial accounting inconsistencies in order to comply with SOX and other key regulations, such as Markets in Financial Instruments Directive (MiFID) and the Revised International Capital Framework (also known as Basel II). Improved auditing technologies and central document management capabilities can help reduce exposure to Sections 302 and 404 of the compliance requirements for SOX.

The dictates of legislation, such as 21 CFR and the Defense Information Systems Agency (DISA) (discussed in Chapter 2), will affect how organizations store and manage electronic information on the desktop and in databases as well as how they manage records and documents down to and including word processing, spreadsheet, and image files.

Chapter Summary

Turning compliance into competitive advantage is a long-term plan for any organization. Compliance undertaken as a proactive step with a vision for the business strategy is a chance to run a better organization. Those that do it well will have a significant competitive advantage.

The components a solid compliance policy (process, governance, culture, information management, and enabling technology) are the same as those required to ensure competitive advantage. Alignment of the compliance requirements with the business vision is essential to achieving benefits within a compliance program. Combining the power of compliance with easy-to-use technologies helps achieve the competitive advantage vision.

Note

1. Del Monte Foods case study, Microsoft Corporation, 2007, www.microsoft.com/casestudies/casestudy.aspx?casestudyid= 4000000699.

Looking For the High Ground

After reading Part III, you will be able to:

- Review some of the trends in governance and compliance.
- Appreciate concerns relating to governance and compliance as global markets change the business landscape.

Businesses are facing new requirements to extend their services to be available worldwide. Under cost pressure, they need to consolidate data centers and business applications and pay attention to new compliance rules and security regulations. The challenge of the twenty-first-century business environment is twofold: complexity and globalization.

Complexity results not only from the number of procedures, rules, and people involved, but also the fact that these people often reside in multiple locations, cultures, and time zones. Managing the rules within one set of societal laws is difficult enough but when multiplied by 5, 10, or even 100, in the case of international entities, it can be overwhelming.

In today's highly competitive and fast-changing markets, global social and business challenges such as water pollution, climate change, and widespread poverty offer huge operating risks as well as great business opportunities. Business leaders who have the vision and are willing to think out of the box can create value for their stakeholders and shareowners, creating new and inimitable sources of competitive advantage.

Our discussion has covered:

- Identifying business risks and opportunities to address environmental and social issues along industry supply chains.

- Grappling with the business reality of managing the corporate response to diverse stakeholders and shareowners in times of economic and political risk.

- Recognizing tools, frameworks, methods, and processes for advancing sustainability for global business success.

- Challenges of aligning business strategy with corporate citizenship and sustainability.

As policies are the why and procedures are the how, compliance risk is often related to procedural execution rather than policy flaws. The challenge, therefore, focuses on procedural codification (the act of mapping the rules to the execution), usage (the interactions with these rules including ensuring understanding and execution behavior), and tracking (the measurement, flows, and patterns of how the rules have been used).

CHAPTER 5

Compliance at the Desktop

After reading this chapter, you will be able to:

- Understand some of the tools available to enable enterprise compliance.
- Examine the issues when considering technology enablement to enhance compliance.
- Identify the elements of information work that influence compliance at the desktop.
- Learn the legal implications of technology enablement.

We have had a good deal of conversation about what is needed so it is now time to focus on how our enterprise can become proactive. This section is a look at what, as leaders and managers, we can reasonably expect to happen at the desktop. In the next few pages we will look at compliance-related tasks using the Information Work (IWork) desktop. Based on our previous conversation regarding the compliance demands for monitoring, measuring, transparency, and risk management, the features you will want to enable include the following:

- Auditing and logging
- Workflow management
- Digital signatures
- Records management
- Classifying e-mail
- Document policies
- Spreadsheet management

EXHIBIT 5.1

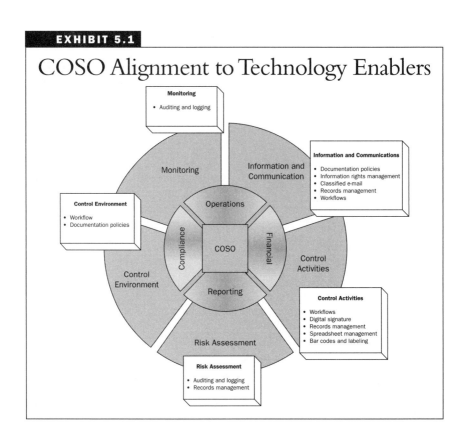

COSO Alignment to Technology Enablers

- Barcodes and labeling
- Information rights management

There are products out there that provide significant versatility because you can use features and settings out of the box without writing any programmatic code. Alternatively, you can extend and customize the features to suit specific business requirements. We will take each of these features in turn, discussing what they are and how, as shown in Exhibit 5.1, they relate back to a basic Committee of Sponsoring Organizations (COSO) compliance framework.

Auditing and Logging

Auditing provides a historical record of actions taken by users so that, when an authentic record is required, you'll know what happened and when it happened. Auditing is required by almost all regulations. For example, the Sarbanes-Oxley Act (SOX) requires that all actions taken on a financial document must be fully audited to meet compliance.

Auditing allows companies to substantiate claims in cases of dispute or litigation. With effective auditing systems, policies, and processes in place, companies have the evidence to support and demonstrate their compliance. Auditing allows authorized users to see all of the people who have accessed resources on a site and what actions those people took.

Tracking key events within a document library and events on a site, such as search, user changes, and changes in content types and columns allows for the creation of good audit trails.

The key challenges in audit trails is first, the collection of data and second, the carefully and logical storage of that data for easy analysis. Creating an audit log, which other applications and systems

EXHIBIT 5.2

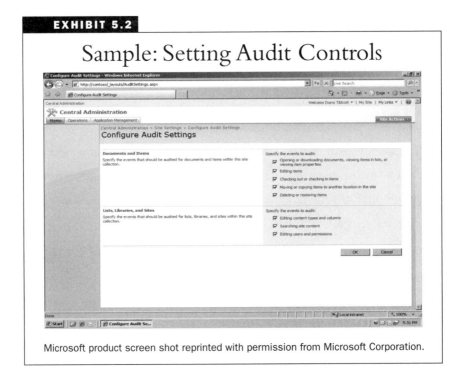

Sample: Setting Audit Controls

Microsoft product screen shot reprinted with permission from Microsoft Corporation.

can use for custom analysis and reporting or for custom auditing, is a key component in proactive measurement. Exhibit 5.2 shows tools to configure audit settings.

Performing Tasks for Auditing

When setting up an audit trail consider some of the following actions as part of the trail:

- Download
- Rename
- Move
- Copy
- Check in/Check out

- New version creation
- Editing of content types and columns
- Search site content
- Edit users and permissions
- Change metadata
- Change policy (document lives in same location, with updated policy)
- Other changes to policy
- Deletion

Your team may find it necessary in some environments to extend the normal "audit" function to address multiple applications (such as validating against the human resources or finance systems). To accomplish this level of integration your technology team will generally need to build some custom connectivity.

Viewing Reports for Auditing

Reports for auditing should allow the administrator to report about specific tasks and modifications the operational team executed during a given period.

The screenshot in Exhibit 5.3 demonstrates a high-level audit report generally used by administrators, who can scan the summary-level information looking for anomalies. Drilling through (clicking on a topic or document) or selecting a detail report would allow the administrator or auditor to view the activity detail.

Exhibit 5.4 shows an example of customized detail auditing designed to view document-level auditing data showing who did what and when.

EXHIBIT 5.3

Sample: Tracking Content

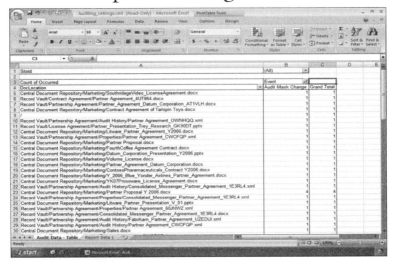

Microsoft product screen shot reprinted with permission from Microsoft Corporation.

EXHIBIT 5.4

Sample: Tracking Content Detail

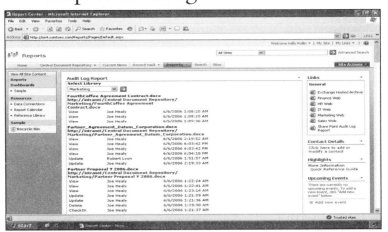

Microsoft product screen shot reprinted with permission from Microsoft Corporation.

Workflow Management

Workflow is the collaborative process by which the various people working on a particular project or task participate and contribute to the activity. Workflow is important to compliance as a way to help ensure that the right information is made available to people at the right time and to enforce procedural rigor on business processes subject to regulatory compliance.

Workflows can help ensure the right people complete their respective tasks in the appropriate sequence (or in parallel) and can make the workflow status visible to others. Because 67 percent of data loss in records management is directly related to user error, automated workflow is integral to the correct, secure, visible, and authentic processing of documents that is required to prove compliance.[1] For example, a company can help defend itself against a lawsuit by proving that all stakeholders have approved the document in question and that their comments and digital signatures have been collected.

A workflow process should notify the next "assigned to" users once the previous user has completed work on the item. Either these users should be able to be assigned in series or in parallel; users have the flexibility to assign the tasks to someone else, if so configured.

Workflow promotes visibility and should display: (1) who the item is assigned to; (2) how long it has been assigned; and (3) what the status is. The administrator is able to view which workflows are currently running on the site, their progress, and their associations.

Workflows should map to important business processes and guide participants through the proper procedure for the work at hand. Workflow capabilities, such as those listed below, facilitate collaboration that is more manageable, enforceable, and measurable business processes, and more intelligent records management. Typical workflows that improve efficiency and promote transparency include:

- Approval
- Collecting feedback
- Collecting signatures
- Disposition approval
- Issue tracking
- Translation management

Once in production, administrators should be able to track each workflow and monitor how it is performing overall, as well as drill down into specific instances of a workflow. For example, with an activity duration report, administrators can see how long each activity in the workflow takes to complete, and how long each instance takes to complete. In a similar manner, a cancellation and error report shows you which workflows are being canceled or are encountering errors before completion.

The workflow capabilities support and, in many cases enforce, the business rules associated with the assigned work. Integration between applications through the workflow can allow users to initiate reviews and approvals without leaving the workflow, simplifying content review and approval processes, and reducing time spent managing documents through their life cycles. In essence, it will design workflows, reinforce business rules, allow nonintrusive audit trails, improve efficiency, and document management. For documents stored in an electronic library with an associated workflow template, users can initiate the workflow process from the desktop client application or from a browser-based interface.

Desktop environments today provide working teams, the ability to associate business logic to items in lists and documents in document libraries to create a custom workflow. New workflow frameworks are flexible so that, for example, you first send a dynamically created e-mail message based on the conditional state of the document or list item. You can add multiple branches and conditions to a workflow so that the business logic is captured, the process is streamlined, and efficiency is increased.

Digital Signatures

Digital signatures are important to compliance as a way to provide assurance that reports are authentic and that the appropriate decision maker or controller duly authorizes approvals and signoffs. A digital signature also improves efficiency by reducing reliance on paper while meeting regulatory requirements. For example, companies in the pharmaceutical and healthcare industries are embracing digital signatures as a way to digitally manage, retrieve, and store official copies of records. A user can now digitally sign a document by using off-the-shelf desktop functionality in products with an extensible signing platform that has an open, standards-based file format.

Signing a Document

Exhibit 5.5 shows the initiation of digitally signing a document.

EXHIBIT 5.5

Sample: Electronic Signature Set-Up

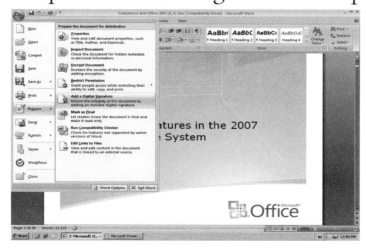

Microsoft product screen shot reprinted with permission from Microsoft Corporation.

TIPS AND TECHNIQUES

Digital Signature

Although the U.S. government has been extremely reluctant to enter into the digital era by allowing the use of digital signatures, proof that progress is being made lies in the fact that after almost seventeen years the International Register of Certified Auditors IRCA[2] enacted new legislation that became effective April 28, 2005, allowing the use of digital signatures and storage of the "Employment Eligibility Verification" (commonly known as the I-9 form). The ability to electronically retain these documents drastically improves the employer's ability to streamline and simplify this tedious process.

Source: Angelo Paparelli, "Driving in the Fast Lane on the Digital I-9 Superhighway," *Immigration Daily,* January, 27, 2005.

You can digitally sign a document for many of the same reasons you might sign a paper document. A digital signature is used to authenticate digital information—such as documents, e-mail messages, and macros—by using computer cryptography. Authentication is the process of verifying that people and products are who and what they claim to be. Digital signatures help to establish the following assurances:

- *Authenticity.* The digital signature helps to assure that the signer is who he or she claims to be. For example, you can confirm the source and integrity of a software publisher's code by verifying the digital signature used to sign the code.

- *Integrity.* The digital signature helps to assure that the content has not been changed or tampered with after it was digitally signed.

- *Nonrepudiation.* The digital signature helps to prove to all parties the origin of the signed content. *Nonrepudiation* means that document signers cannot later deny that they were the ones who signed the content.

E-Signatures Streamline Paper-Bound Processes

An electronic signature is certainly an excellent means to explore the options of the paperless office. Human Resources organizations might consider using this technique with their package of 'onboarding' documents issued by their hiring staff including:

- Job applications
- Offer letters
- I-9 Forms

- Employee Handbook Acknowledgements
- Employment agreements

This is especially enticing as more businesses engage virtual and telecommuting workers. The organization taking this path will want to clearly understand some key regulations relating to electronic signature in the countries in which they operate. In the United States this would include: the federal Electronic Signatures in Global and National Commerce Act (the E-Sign Act), the Uniform Electronic Transactions Action (UETA) and the regulations governing the use of electronic signatures on I-9 (INS rules) and W-4 (IRS rules) forms.

To be in compliance with the E-Sign Act and UETA, the organization should, among other things, use an "electronic signature" that has the following:

- An electronic symbol, sound or process must be associated with the record and

- The sound, symbol, or process must be executed or adopted by the person with the intent to sign the record.

Essentially, it must be clear to the person making the authorization that they are intending to 'sign' the document in questions.[3]

Signature Criteria

To make these assurances, the content creator must digitally sign the content by using a signature that satisfies the following criteria:

- *The digital signature is valid.* Valid refers to the status of a certificate checked against a certificate authority database and found to be legitimate. Legitimate means the certificate is current, not expired or revoked. Documents signed by a valid certificate and not altered since signing are considered valid.

- *The certificate associated with the digital signature is current (not expired).* A certificate is a digital means of proving identity and authenticity. Certificates are provided by a certification authority, and like a driver's license, can expire or be revoked.

- *The signing person or organization, known as the publisher, is trusted.* Trust is an indication of whether you trust the individual or group for whom the certificate is provided. The default setting is Inherit Trust from Issuer, which means that the certificate is trusted because the issuer, usually a certificate authority, is trusted.

- *The certificate associated with the digital signature is provided to the signing publisher by a reputable certificate authority (CA).* A CA is usually a commercial organization that issues digital certificates, keeps track of who is assigned to a certificate, signs certificates to verify their validity, and tracks which certificates are revoked or expired.

Applications supporting digital signature, as shown in Exhibit 5.6, can detect these criteria for you and alert you if there is a problem with the digital signature.

Signatures can be captured as images, as shown in Exhibit 5.7, and used during the digital signing process. The ability to capture digital signatures and inserting them electronically on signature lines in documents makes it possible for organizations to step into the paperless office dream by using the paperless signing processes for documents such as contracts, internal compliance validations, order forms, and other agreements.

EXHIBIT 5.6

Sample: Record of Valid Digital Signature

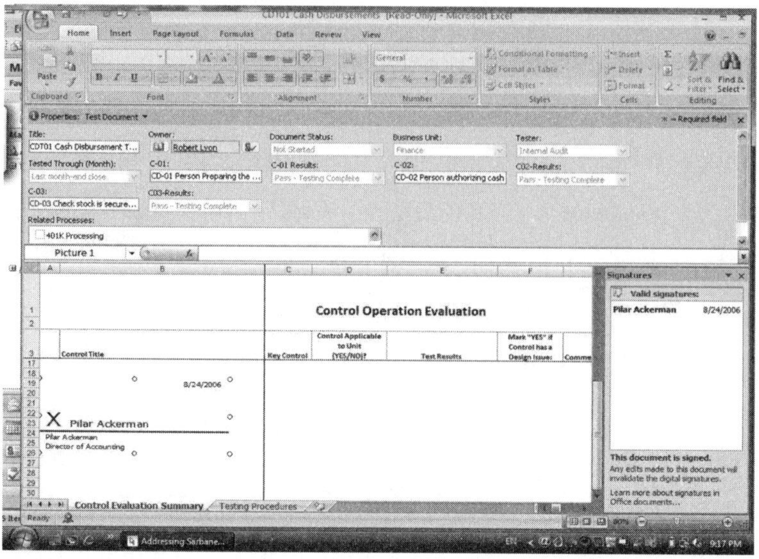

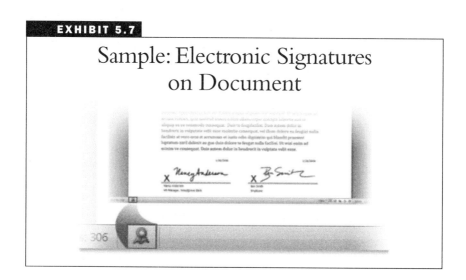

Microsoft product screen shot reprinted with permission from Microsoft Corporation.

EXHIBIT 5.7

Sample: Electronic Signatures on Document

Two advantages that digital signature lines offer are that—unlike signatures on paper—they can provide a record of exactly what was signed and they allow the signature to be verified in the future. After a document has been digitally signed, it can become a read-only document to prevent modifications.

Records Management

A common element in compliance regulations is the requirement to securely archive records for long periods of time in a safe and unalterable state. The ability to archive documents is just one component of a larger records management process that includes the collection, management, and expiration of corporate records (information important for the history, knowledge, or legal defense of a company) in a consistent and uniform manner based on a company's policies. Electronically enforceable business rules can help companies ensure that vital corporate records, including critical documents, are properly retained for legal, compliance, and business purposes and then properly disposed of when no longer needed. The application and structure of this collection-management-security cycle are depicted graphically in Exhibit 5.8 and described in the following discussion.

Records management for a large organization requires scalable and efficient management components including these critical areas of focus:

- *Content security* such as the records management applications should have several features to help ensure content security for the document libraries and files stored within it. Records should never be automatically modified by the system. In

EXHIBIT 5.8

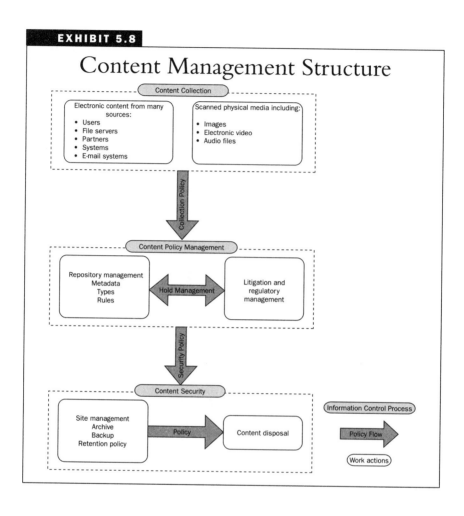

Content Management Structure

other words, records stored in the repository and the copies downloaded by the users should always be identical, byte for byte. The repository should have security settings to reduce the possibility that users and/or administrators might directly (within the repository) modify the records. This security can be provided by strict version control on any changes made to document contents and by auditing specific types of changes.

Additionally, the repository application should allow administrators to manage only the record-level metadata. Record-level metadata should always be maintained separately from the content metadata. This allows an audit of who managed (moved, added, etc.) the items in the repository. Changes to this "external" metadata can be audited as well, which is especially important for compliance with regulations such as 21 CFR Part 11 to ensure that enterprises can report exactly how they've used particular types of content such as patient data.

- *Content management policy* such as policy enforcement rules, item retention and holds in response to external events, and content expiration. These policies provide controls that consistently and uniformly enforce the labeling, auditing, and expiration of records. The records management application should allow the administrator to configure policies for a specific storage location or content type. For example, to ensure that all contracts are retained uniformly in an organization, their expiration dates can be based on a common property such as the contract execution date.

- *Content collection policies* including allowed content types such as spreadsheets, documents, and e-mail. Records management applications provide a company with a set of services that support both the electronic collection and collection policies that govern the repository. These policies allow users as well as other systems to easily submit content to the repository even if they do not have direct access or permission to any of the repository contents. Many systems allow submission via a Web service or through an e-mail message.

- *Record routing.* When content is submitted to a records center site, it can be routed to its proper location within the records management system based on its content type.

- *Content types and routing.* To maintain compliance, companies must ensure that hundreds of thousands of employees follow complex and sometimes inconvenient procedures for managing documents and other content to ensure that records subject to compliance regulations are complete, accurate, secure, and available.

FROM THE REAL WORLD

Metadata

New amendments to the Federal Rules of Civil Procedure (FRCP) that became effective December 1, 2006, have brought organizations to a crossroads in the way they deal with the issues raised by metadata in civil litigation. These new amendments update traditional discovery rules for the modern era of electronic documents and force organizations and their legal teams to consider the impact of electronic data, including hidden data associated with documents, in every case.

One of the biggest difficulties in managing content in a large organization is making sure that everyone understands and follows corporate policies, such as managing out-of-date information or requiring labels so that paper copies can be traced back to electronic originals. Establishing robust information management policies that let site administrators and list managers control how content is managed is critical to records management system success. Thus far, we have focused on document management policies; the same standards can be applied to other types of content, such as pictures, list items, and third-party content.

Predefined content tags can allow you to predefine metadata boilerplates so that all newly created documents of a given type automatically have appropriate metadata such as workflow, resulting actions, expiration, and other policies. Content types address a significant obstacle to automating better compliance: the lack of information classification. If the system regards all content as plain "documents," then the system can't enforce policies such as expiration according to the type of content. For example: As demonstrated in Exhibit 5.9, when using content tagging, the system can tell the difference between "issues" and "control" documents and automatically enforce different policies (such as read-only status or validating the users right to read the content) according to those content types.

Information classification has represented a significant roadblock to compliance automation. A number of products today provide the capability of presetting metadata (content tags) as content is added to the repository. Enforcing content policies, such as expatriation dates and administrative rights, can become an automated process managed by business rules.

Example: In one company, all contracts may have a shelf life of seven years, but issues documents may require retention for only three years unless tagged for litigation retention.

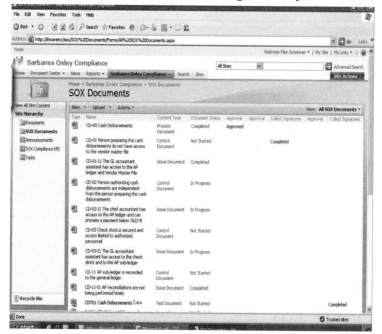

Microsoft product screen shot reprinted with permission from Microsoft Corporation.

Pretagging Content

Many repositories suffer with user apathy. Getting users to submit content is one of the greatest challenges for knowledge (or content) managers. When users do submit content, getting them to tag it properly and fully is a huge content management challenge. Smart repository management tools now provide something close to "automated" metadata tagging. In these advanced repository environments, when a user clicks *New* in a document library to create (or submit) a new file, they are generally asked to select a content type. Based on the selected content type, the metadata properties are automatically associated with the new document. For example, you can create a premade proposal content type that captures relevant attributes (such as customer, product type, and salesperson) for each sales proposal.

Several benefits arise from ensuring metadata inclusion at the time of documentation creation.

- Finding documents is much easier thanks to the abundance of metadata. For example, in the case of proposals, you can easily search and retrieve all proposals associated with a specific product type, salesperson, or date.

- Content submitted to a repository can be routed to the proper location within the records management system based on metadata tags.

No benefit comes without some effort. Pretagging mechanisms are wonderful but require administrators to initially load, and routinely update, content management policies. These policies must be clearly outlined, managed, and reviewed to remain in compliance with current governance and regulatory standards.

As part of any records management content policy, the systems should provide for authorized users (such as information technology [IT] staff, records managers, and legal authorities) to apply one or more holds that suspend records management policies on specific items to prevent documents from being changed during litigation, audits, or other investigations. The process of creating, managing, and releasing holds needs to be monitored and recorded so that the system can account for all actions taken.

Reaping the Benefits

The SOX documents shown in Exhibit 5.9 show the administrator not only the title, format, and status but the content type (in column 3). If required, the administrator could produce a listing of all approved Issues Documents or Approved Process Documents for a given year and cycle.

E-mail Message Record Management

E-mail, as a document-generation mechanism, has long represented a records management challenge. Enterprise e-mail systems today should allow administrators to create managed e-mail environments that get pushed out to users who have the option of opting into specific situations based on their job functions. These e-mail folders have policies associated with them that define things like the retention period and quota for the content of these folders. Using rules within centralized enterprise e-mail systems, such as Exchange Server 2007, you can set up these folders to send e-mail messages to a records management site. Many systems today will allow users to simply drag and drop an e-mail from their inbox into the appropriate managed e-mail folder, and any required metadata can be entered asynchronously into the records management site.

The following list provides some insight into the number of the primary regulatory body or regulation that applies to e-mail retention.

Industry Impact	Regulation
Banking	FDIC (Federal Deposit Insurance Corporation), OCC (Office of the Comptroller of the Currency)
Telecommunications	Title 47, Part 42
Pharmaceutical	FDA (Food and Drug Administration)—Title 21, Part 11
Healthcare	HIPAA (Health Insurance Portability and Accountability Act)
Defense	DoD (Department of Defense)—5015.2 standard
Brokerage firms	SEC (Securities and Exchange Commission)—Rules 17a-3 and 17a-4
General business oversight	Sarbanes-Oxley Act (contains provisions for record retention and audits)

Classifying E-mail

IT organizations need to provide users with a way to mark up messages with an outgoing classification. Certain industries have specific regulations for which mail classifications would satisfy their requirements. An example of a broad regulation that is aided by e-mail classifications is the Health Insurance Portability and Accountability Act of 1996 (HIPAA) requirement to let users know that they are receiving messages that communicate benefits. Any message receiving the "Benefits Communication" policy then needs to be processed by the company (on behalf of the employee) with specific rules and regulations. For example, the employee has permission to know everyone that received a copy.

New options in e-mail systems allow central IT organizations to distribute a set of e-mail classifications that users can use to communicate the rules or behaviors that they should be subject to while reading the e-mail.

FROM THE REAL WORLD

The Health Insurance Portability and Accountability Act (HIPAA) of 1996 is a broad and comprehensive set of regulations requiring health care organizations to address privacy and security concerns related to electronically stored and transmitted health care data. The HIPAA's Security Rule mandates technical safeguards and further details the security standards to be implemented by organizations for the protection of electronic data. Although the Security Rule provides covered entities with implementation specifications describing how the standards are to be implemented, HIPAA is designed to be technology neutral. Individual organizations must make the decision on which technology solutions allow the organization to comply with HIPAA requirements. Accordingly, wireless devices are not specifically detailed in HIPAA's Security Rule but must be viewed in the context of the health care organization's entire system for electronically storing and transmitting data.

Source: J. Tikkanen, JJT Consulting Group, "BlackBerry and Health Insurance Portability and Accountability Act (HIPAA) Guidelines," white paper.

Sample configurable policies may include:

- *Attorney/Client Privileged:* "This message is privileged and recipients are instructed to [take whatever action is described]."

- *Benefits Communication:* "This message originated from your benefits department and under HIPAA regulations."

- *HR Communication:* "This message contains confidential and sensitive information."

When using an e-mail system that permits the application of classification rules when a classified e-mail message is received by a user, it will contain exactly the same banner that was shown to the author when the message was created. This application of classification rules provides the user with critical compliance information about what type of message this is or how to behave while reading this message.

Classification rules can be used to reduce intellectual property risk, including:

- Controlling the dissemination of sensitive data through the circulation of printed copies. In such a case, you will want to limit the printing of certain documents to a specific set of highly secure, access-controlled printers. You can achieve this goal as well through use of another central IT rule.

- Long-term record preservation; specifically, ensuring that your electronic files are in a format that can be read 15 to 20 years from today.

Using content management policies and rules, the administrator can create a policy that generates a fixed-format copy of the content, and assign it to the content types designated for preservation. Then, for each document of that content type, the policy feature creates a fixed format rendering of the document and stores it in the repository. If the repository program provides for automatic enforcement, all items subject to the policy will be secured, with no intervention required from records managers or IT.

Litigation Support

Compliance rules can determine how long to keep data and dictate what data is produced on demand for regulatory authorities. However, litigation support finds and produces whatever data the company has that relates to the legal issue at hand. Litigation support includes broad document discovery that cannot be specified beforehand as to what data may be relevant. The requirements for compliance and litigation-risk reduction, however, do overlap.

Do not look at the e-mail archive as a litigation case management tool. E-mail archives can feed into a larger litigation case management plan but should be considered a replacement for it.

Litigation case management requirements should include:

- Litigation destruction-hold features:
  - Applying an indefinite destruction hold to the archive or portions of the archive.
  - Applying targeted destruction holds, based on flexible criteria that result from a search, to narrowly target the hold to items specific to the response.
  - Allowing multiple destruction holds against one item.
  - Releasing an individual destruction hold against one item, while leaving any others in place.
  - Applying a friendly name to destruction holds, such as a case name or number.
  - Providing a reporting function, or dashboard, for the destruction-hold function.

- Search and retrieval features:

  - A robust search engine that allows searches by a number of criteria and methodologies. The search engine should meet the requirements of all involved in discovery efforts.

  - Retrieval options for writing the results to the location and media of choice. For example, a specific file location on any network-accessible drive, CD, or DVD.

  - Search and retrieval documentation that is adequate to fulfill any chain-of-custody requirements from regulators, courts, or opposing parties.

  - Search and retrieval performance that meets the timeliness requirements for document production. Examples include response to regulatory requirements or the Federal Rules of Civil Procedure.

  - Search-term lists that can be imported without having to manually retype them.

  - Full-text indexing of all items as they are archived.

  - Integration with the case-management tool of choice.

  - Encryption capabilities.

- Audit trail features:

  - Developing audit trails for all accesses, search-and-retrieval actions, and disposition activity.

  - Documenting the chain of custody.

  - Hiding audit logs and destruction holds from end users who are subject to investigation.

- Printing a summary of the retention schedule for the archive. The summary may include all the retention rules in force, categorized by criteria such as group and job level. It may also include a change history of those rules.
- Storing audit logs, including the retention schedule, as items in the e-mail archive.
- Security and access control features:
  - Inheriting the access controls that archived items had in the e-mail system.
  - Applying special processing to items marked with security classifications, such as confidential or attorney-client privileged communication.
  - Reducing risk means making sure that all e-mail is diverted to known, manageable locations.
  - Keeping the complete archive in one spot. Ensuring that the company has reasonable assurance that all e-mail messages are deleted according to policy.

The bottom line is that companies need to think carefully about the e-mail-archiving features they choose, using a top-down approach. Every company has its own unique set of required features based on its goals and policies. Systems will vary based on the goals of each enterprise.

Managing Holds

A number of compliance regulations mandate that organizations be able to produce records required by investigations and court discovery actions. Failure to fulfill such requests in a timely and complete fashion can expose the company and its officials to liability. Even the inadvertent destruction of records can create criminal liability issues.

Although many companies would like to preserve content only as long as they absolutely have to, events such as litigation require that relevant content be maintained for the lifespan of that event, even if it exceeds the normal lifespan of the item. If records are subjected to multiple audits or litigations, those records must be maintained until the last litigation or audit is completed. To meet this need, use a hold feature designed to respond to events by associating records with these events and overriding the expiration policy of these records appropriately to ensure that they cannot be deleted manually or automatically during the lifespan of the events.

By default, every records repository should be provisioned with a hold list in which each item corresponds to a single hold order. The list provides tools for finding and holding relevant records, viewing the records currently on a hold, and releasing the hold after the hold order is no longer active. When an event such as a discovery motion occurs, a records manager, lawyer, or IT administrator defines a new hold by adding an item to the hold list. The item specifies a name for the hold event, a description, and the person responsible for managing the hold.

The next step in responding to the hold order is to suspend the policies on all relevant records that may be scattered across different document types and stores. An established metadata enhanced search function makes it easy to find relevant records.

Legal staff should be able to view a list of all records currently being held for a specific hold event. After the hold order is no longer in effect (e.g., because the underlying litigation matter has been resolved), the records manager can release the hold order. This should automatically resume normal enforcement of policies on all records that were previously subject to this hold order. In the event that a record is subject to more than one hold, it will not revert to its original policy enforcement until all of its hold events are resolved.

Spreadsheet Management

The Sarbanes-Oxley Act focuses on integrity and accuracy of financial reporting by publicly held companies. However, most publicly traded companies use spreadsheets to aggregate financial numbers from various divisions and applications for producing financial reports. The financial and logistics applications that generate these numbers incorporate numerous controls to ensure accuracy, completeness, and integrity. But after these numbers make it into a spreadsheet, there is no way to ensure the integrity of the spreadsheet data and formulas.

Sending spreadsheets through e-mail messages or even storing them on a file server is a major challenge for companies struggling to maintain financial compliance. When users open a spreadsheet, they can see everything—all sheets, all calculations, and even hidden cells. They are able to arbitrarily change formulas and values and then forward the spreadsheet to other people. This can result in multiple versions of the spreadsheet and no assurance as to the integrity of the calculations or transparency as to who changed what. Spreadsheets are a pain point for companies that need to comply with strict regulations stating that all financial documents must be secure, have integrity, and be completely audited.

Using web-based distribution has several advantages over desktop application alone. First, by being posted to a web part, all viewers can see it in a centralized location where the original, posted document is protected from unauthorized changes. Users can download a copy of the spreadsheet and experiment with it, but they cannot modify the original, official version of the document, which becomes part of the company's official business record. As a result, there is one version of the spreadsheet for a company's financial data. Authors can make cells editable so that an individual can perform calculations and models for themselves.

Authors can also select which objects (such as a chart or a list) or worksheets they want to be made public, as shown in Exhibit 5.10. Calculations can be hidden so that all private and confidential information is not exposed.

EXHIBIT 5.10

Sample: Web-based Content Presentation

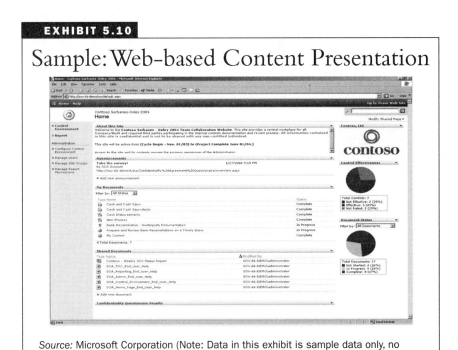

Source: Microsoft Corporation (Note: Data in this exhibit is sample data only, no information is included that is related to a real company.)

Bar Codes and Labeling

So far, we have focused on many forms of documents, including spreadsheets, e-mails, and memos, but much critical business content is essentially nondigital assets. If paper, Mylar, or other physical content is not properly managed, companies face potential loss of records due to misfiling, or the lack of workflow history, audit history, version history, or comments. Nondigital content often falls through the cracks of automated compliance controls and, if mishandled, can expose the organization to liability.

The functionality around policy and records management is evolving rapidly. We are now looking at documents and records management systems with the capability to generate and embed bar codes and labels within documents. Text-based labels or bar codes can be generated from document metadata, such as subject keywords or customer numbers. Labels and bar codes are automatically printed with the document.

Bar codes enable users to manage physical items (such as printouts of documents) by linking those items back to corresponding items in the repository. Companies can affix an identifier to a physical item and then associate that identifier to any document or item in the repository.

Information Rights Management

Confidentiality and integrity are central elements of most compliance regulations but it is very difficult to control what individuals do with copies of electronic documents. It is easy for people to send copies outside the organization or make unauthorized, untraceable modifications.

With information rights management (IRM), you can address these compliance risks by protecting and maintaining greater control over digital information, including confidential and sensitive documents. IRM should allow you to set policies to control that can open, copy, print, or forward information created.

Specific features to look for in IRM technology include:

- *Information rights management* that enables users to define exactly who can open, modify, print, forward, and take other actions with the information.
- *Policy statements.* Establish policy statements for specific e-mail message types and embed these statements in the message. Policy statements can instruct the reader how to handle the message content or serve as a flag to trigger the operating system to process custom-defined rules.

We have always just used access control lists (ACLs)—why not continue?

The limitation of ACLs is that they limit access only at the server. After someone downloads a document, ACLs cannot control whether a person with the rights to a document sends it to someone who does not have rights. IRM, however, works by encrypting the file and limiting the set of users and applications that are allowed to decrypt the file. It can also limit the rights of users who are allowed to read the file, so that they cannot print copies or copy text.

Although there is no technical way to prevent people from divulging sensitive information, IRM helps by restricting who can access sensitive documents and what people can do with these documents after opening them. Moreover, policy statements can help reinforce end-user responsibility by ensuring that end users know that information is sensitive, thus eliminating the "ignorance" defense in the event of a disclosure.

Using Document Information

Compliance requirements, such as fulfilling requests for business records, often require you to find all records associated with a specific project, product, accounts, department, customer, vendor or other characteristic(s). Simple keywords searches often do not turn up adequate results.

Documents created or managed within a records management system contain what is called metadata. Metadata is the data carried in the document wrapper that identifies key pieces of information about the document, such as the author, date of creation or last edit, or topics. The records management system collects and retrieves metadata to give context to the document and increase the ability to search for it.

For example, if the content management system is instructed to pick up the status of the document, then as soon as the document status changes on the system, the metadata changes.

Metadata is captured and is a less intrusive way to collect desired information from users. With today's improved search capabilities, this metadata can be used to index and group results more accurately and associate documents with a set of customers, products, and related documents. A well structured storage and retrieval framework, as outlined in Exhibit 5.11, will help to ensure the greatest benefit from both your content and the portal that houses it.

Portal Search

Many compliance regulations require that companies publish only up-to-the-minute and approved data sets. Under SOX, for example, financial reporting must be accurate and disclosed on a timely basis, which requires the right people to have the right information at the right time. To comply, users must first find information—the right information and all the information related to a specific issue. Information related to a court case or other matter may be scattered across multiple systems, including enterprise resource planning (ERP) systems, servers, and other databases and applications.

Intra- and internet portal products have integrated search engines that use search algorithms to return fast and relevant search results. Portal search allows you to find identical copies of documents, and you can search against unstructured and structured information simultaneously. Users can find information, as shown in Exhibit 5.9, not only from internal content repositories but also from multiple other sources, such as ERP systems and file shares, by using advanced, full-text search from within their integrated organizational portal. This search can include results for different file types and data sources using extensibility mechanisms, and can find not only information and data but also the relevant people who are experts in the search topics. These experts are found and organized by their degrees of separation from the user, based on the user's known contacts. Making good use of metadata information (as discussed above), search is improved and can provide instant access to critical documents.

EXHIBIT 5.11

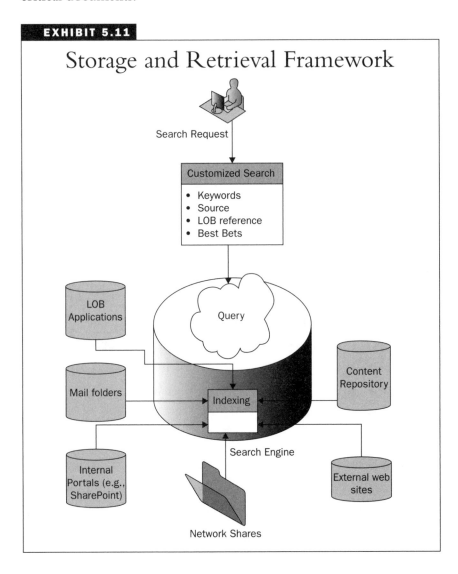

Storage and Retrieval Framework

Improving Compliance with Technology

This section highlights principal areas where technology can help to fill compliance requirements, and it maps each of these areas to the five common regulatory compliance requirements discussed earlier in this document.

Viewing Item-Level Audit History

The audit log contains information about when a user opens or downloads a file, views items in a list, views item properties, edits items, checks items in or out, moves or copies files to another location in the site, and deletes or restores a file. All of this information can be written to a content database, where an administrator can view all of the auditing history for the entire site.

Alternatively, you can write the query results to a spreadsheet, which can then be published to a portal.

Managing Instant Messaging History to a Records Management

A major issue of compliance is handling unstructured data such as e-mail and instant messaging. The records management system should provide you with the ability to connect to and send all instant messaging session history to the repository.

Signing of Documents

Authenticity is a major issue in compliance. Digital signatures help ensure authenticity and signed documents can then be stored centrally. Users should be able to upload a document to a portal, the user should be able to then digitally sign that file during the upload process to ensure that all necessary files are authenticated. Your system could then verify the key and store it in a protected document library.

Using Information Rights Management with Classifications for Advanced E-mail Protection

A user can specify a set of rights and permissions that allow an e-mail message or document to be opened or downloaded only by an authorized individual or group of individuals. In addition, a user can specify whether an e-mail message or document can be printed, forwarded, or copied. Some systems will allow e-mail classification to further notify users about the discretion of the message. For example, an administrator can create a classification where a user can mark a message as "Patient Confidential" or "Company Confidential." This classification adds another level of security information.

Tracking of Changes to Document

Centralized auditing can be used in many managed repositories so that all events that occur within repository (or portal site) are audited. Though the central repository can look for and manage events that occur to documents stored in it, it cannot manage what happens to a downloaded document. For example, the central repository cannot guard against a document being printed, changed, or edited (such as calculations in a spreadsheet), copied, or sent in an e-mail message.

But some system will provide your company with ways to implement full audit on any file that resides in its repository or on a portal site. To accomplish this task, you could seek to capture user actions after a user downloads a file from the server. Either incrementally or whenever certain events are triggered, you could pass the event information (audit trail) on the to the audit log.

Mapping Opportunities Summary

The checks in the table indicate which scenarios required or applicable to support compliance with various regulations we have discussed.

	Audit—at the item/detail level	Audit—Client-side	E-mail—IRM Protected Classified	IM Record History	Server-side Signing
SOX	Recommended Use	Recommended Use	N/A	Recommended Use (specifically for financial reporting & in clinical studies)	Recommended Use
HIPPA	Useful	Useful	Required for patient information	Useful	Useful
GLBA	Recommended Use	Recommended Use	Useful	Useful	Useful
Basel II	Useful	Useful	N/A	Useful	Useful

(Continued)

	Audit—at the item/detail level	Audit—Client-side	E-mail—IRM Protected Classified	IM Record History	Server-side Signing
SEC	Recommended Use	Useful	Useful	Recommended Use	Useful
21CFR	Recommended Use	Useful	N/A	N/A	Useful
DoD 5015.2	Recommended Use	Useful	Useful	Useful	N/A
ISO	Required for RM	Useful	Useful	N/A	Useful

Chapter Summary

Turning compliance into competitive advantage is a long-term plan for any organization. Compliance undertaken as a proactive step with a vision for the business strategy is a chance to run a better organization. Those that do it well will have a significant competitive advantage.

The components of a solid compliance policy (process, governance, culture, information management, and enabling technology) are the same as those required to ensure effective and efficient operations. As with any program within an organization, alignment of the compliance requirements with the business vision is essential to achieving benefit. Embedding compliance, not only in the organization culture but within the infrastructure by utilizing the power of easy-to-use technologies forges a strong link between work, strategy, and delivery.

Notes

1. Comments from Craig Rhinehart, Microsoft ILM Summit 2006.

2. About IRCA: The International Register of Certificated Auditors (IRCA) is the world's original and largest international certification body for auditors of management systems. Located in the UK in the center of London, IRCA certifies more than 13,750 auditors in over 120 countries worldwide, www.irca.org/about/about.html.

3. Summarized from "Signing on the Electronic Line: The Developing Law of E-Signatures" by William E. Hannum III and Shannon Lynch.

CHAPTER 6

Powering Compliance

After reading this chapter, you will be able to:

- Relate trends in compliance enablement.
- Connect key legislation to enterprise compliance challenges.

Many companies face increasing pressure to comply with governmental regulations for handling business and personal information. These regulations are designed to protect against a diverse array of risks that span different industries, disciplines, and government agencies. Reasons for increased regulations include:

- The stories of corporate scandals involving large companies and government agencies have resulted in an increase in the number and scope of compliance regulations intended to protect shareholders and improve the visibility, integrity, and accountability of financial reporting.

- Concerns about the privacy of individuals and the possible abuse of personal information have prompted regulations for handling health care information.

- Risks related to food supplies and to the development of pharmaceuticals have prompted increased regulation for all industries regulated by the U.S. Food and Drug Administration (FDA).

- The surge in identity theft and fraud has prompted regulations for handling personal identifiable information and informing consumers when their personal information is disclosed inappropriately.

In the United States, compliance legislation designed to address these risks affects most publicly traded companies, the health care industry, government agencies, and financial institutions. Governments impose severe penalties for violations against compliance regulation laws, including major fines and imprisonment of company officials. In our discussion we outlined examples of penalties for violating certain regulations such as the Health Insurance Portability and Accountability Act (HIPAA) regulations that range from $100 per person per incident for improper disclosures of health information to $250,000 and 10 years in prison for intentional violations (United States Department of Health and Human Services, May 2003). Noncompliance can also have a negative effect on a company's reputation in the market or elected officials to govern.

Enterprises stand the best chance of success when they go beyond viewing compliance as overhead and take the opportunity to streamline and improve core business processes as part of their compliance efforts. This is because much of what is contained in current compliance regulations are long-recognized best practices. Many companies not subject to certain compliance regulations are taking the initiative to follow some regulations anyway, because of the value both in operations and reputation. For example, ISO 9000, which is a set of standards around manufacturing process quality, requires good records management so that a company can demonstrate compliance. There are important reputation and financial benefits for companies to comply with that standard, even if there aren't specific fines for noncompliance (ISO 9000 is a voluntary standard). A "follow the spirit of the law" approach (as opposed to "letter of the law") not only tends to improve compliance scores, but also helps companies get value from their investment in compliance.

Companies must develop long-term compliance strategies to meet the requirements established by government regulations. Typically, these strategies involve formalizing compliance policies and implementing specific business processes to support, enforce, and demonstrate compliance with these policies. Unless information technology (IT) is involved in automating these processes, a company risks being overwhelmed with a manual documentation effort and a weak control infrastructure. A major challenge is how to interpret compliance regulations and map them to IT implementations that use existing IT investments—investments that were often deployed before the rise of compliance requirements.

Recapping Key Compliance Regulations

Companies must comply with these key regulations:

- *Sarbanes-Oxley Act (SOX) (United States, 2002)*. A set of U.S. federal laws that establish new or enhanced standards for all U.S. publicly traded company boards, management, and public accounting firms. The act contains 11 titles that affect corporate governance, financial disclosure, and public accounting practices.

- *Data Protection Act (European Union, 1998)*. A British act of Parliament that provides a legal basis for the privacy and protection of data. The act states that data collected by one party to another party may be used only for the specific purposes for which it was collected. Personal data may be kept only for an appropriate length of time and must not be disclosed to other parties without the consent of the data owner.

- *Health Insurance Portability and Accountability Act (HIPAA) (United States, 1996)*. A set of U.S. federal laws that improve the efficiency and effectiveness of the health care system. HIPAA encourages the development of a health information system through the establishment of standards and requirements for the electronic transmission of certain health information. The act aims to improve the portability and continuity of health insurance coverage in the group and individual markets; to combat waste, fraud, and abuse in health insurance and health care delivery; to promote the use of medical savings accounts; to improve access to long-term care services and coverage; to simplify the administration of health insurance; and to achieve other purposes.

- *Title 21 Code of Federal Regulations (21 CFR Part 11) (United States, 1997).* A set of life sciences regulations that affect how biotechnology and pharmaceutical companies meet the criteria for acceptance by the U.S. Food and Drug Administration. The FDA considers under certain circumstances that electronic records, electronic signatures, and handwritten signatures executed to electronic records are equivalent to paper records and handwritten signatures executed on paper. These regulations, which apply to all FDA program areas, are intended to permit the widest possible use of electronic technology, compatible with the FDA's responsibility to promote and protect public health.

- *Basel Capital Accord (Basel II) (Switzerland, 2004).* Basel II affects banks and other financial institutions by defining capital requirements for banks' exposures to certain trading-related activities, including counterparty credit risk, and for the treatment of double-default effects (the risk that both a borrower and guarantor default on the same obligation).

Common Compliance Requirements

Although these regulations vary in terms of scope, intent, and type of information, they all share common elements and rely on the fundamental principles of information security:

- *Confidentiality.* Confidential, personal, and sensitive information cannot be exposed to unauthorized organizations or individuals.

- *Integrity.* Data cannot be modified by unauthorized organizations or individuals, and the completeness and accuracy must be insured.

- *Availability.* Information must be available to the right people at the right time to support timely and accurate financial reporting and to fulfill demands for information by regulators, investigators, and court subpoenas.

Organizations must implement policies and procedures to make sure individual and departmental activities conform to compliance requirements. However, only publishing policies and procedures and buying technologies to ensure confidentiality, integrity, and availability falls short of compliance. An organization must exercise due diligence in enforcing the execution of those policies and procedures.

Procedural Rigor

An organization risks becoming quickly bogged down if executives and managers must manually enforce procedural rigor and workers must perform busy work mandated by a bureaucracy created out of compliance requirements. Good workflow automation enforces compliance and performance of business processes and policies as unobtrusively and automatically as possible.

To support audits and investigations, an organization must also be able to prove that it performed compliance procedures when needed and that its technology controls were active and they performed throughout the period in question. This requirement creates a documentation burden on top of other work associated with compliance policies. This documentation burden creates a need for IT involvement.

Auditing and Logging

Auditing and logging trace how individuals access and use resources and execute business procedures. Systems that process sensitive data must securely log, maintain, and provide critical event information to ensure a clear audit trail.

Audit trails and logging are especially important for two of the pillars of information security. First, audit trails are crucial in determining the scope of disclosures of confidential information. Being able to reconstruct who accessed what information and when allows an organization to inform just the people whose information was compromised, sometimes greatly reducing the fines and other costs that are in direct proportion to the quantity of individuals whose information was compromised. Second, logging facilitates integrity controls. Technology may not always be able to prevent an authorized user from maliciously or inadvertently modifying information, but an audit trail provides a control and allows the organization to understand the impact of the incident. For example, it is not enough to point to a written policy that governs how financial spreadsheets and their formulas are maintained. Compliance and audit professionals want to see an audit trail of changes to such spreadsheets that shows who accessed them, what was modified, and when.

The Compliance Technology Landscape

Operational compliance solutions are a mix of process, procedure, and technology enablement. Well-balanced proactive and long-term solutions utilize a combination of streamlined processes and existing investments and are supported by the internal enterprise, partner, and customer ecosystem.

Looking at Solutions

Long-term proactive solutions include software components, templates, and governance guidance that allow customers and partners to implement a wide variety of compliance requirements across financial, human resources, and production processes.

Well-articulated compliance solutions that can help organizations facilitate compliance initiatives while providing business benefits include: visibility into processes, risks, and controls; an easier and accelerated compliance process; and a flexible foundation that adapts to customers' needs and longer-term compliance initiatives regardless of locality.

Operational compliance, whether for SOX, Basel II, or other regulations, call for information clarity that comes only from rapid, clear, and transparent communications. Many features to look for are outlined in Exhibit 6.1.

Utilizing Existing Technology Investments

Start by looking at your existing environment. If possible extend the life of your current investments by building on existing functionality, such as using digital rights management associated with your current e-mail system or an approval workflow feature that comes with your current portal application. These changes can improve compliance by leveraging existing processes and technology. This approach makes it is easier for the general employee base to become

EXHIBIT 6.1

Feature–Functionality Outline

Enabling Feature	Definition/Use
Content (documents, images, and other electronic information) Management	• Defines document types (e.g., process, risk, control, and test) and properties for each. • Generates documents with reusable forms and templates. • Associate documents in parent-child fashion. • Migrate and utilize existing control documentation. • Use the COSO framework or custom-control methodologies based on accepted accounting principles. • Use Extensible Markup Language (XML) to capture and report document properties. • Store reference materials in a shared document repository. • Capture and report document modifications with audit-trail features.
Workflows	• Customizable workflow steps to support various document types. • Dynamically add/subtract users and tasks from workflows (e.g., route document to another worker for further action). • Allow workers to move back or forward within the workflow. • Allow for role and user based security access to information. • Provide personal tasks lists for user (such as My Tasks).
Collaboration and Communication	• Provide for information sharing and collaborative work on intra-internet-based team spaces with presence and multi-channel communications. • Version control and check-in/check-out features for all content regardless of type or format. • Audit and usage report capabilities for all content. • E-mail notification of repository changes (new documents, modifications, and deletions).
Repository Reporting and Monitoring	• Status reporting for content (completed, in progress, not started, etc.) and graphical user effectiveness ratings (such as not rated, effective, not effective). • Document data (such as type, location, status, control effectiveness, and owner). • Export data to spreadsheet or database for further analysis. • Print summary and detailed reports. • Custom reporting on all meta data (searchable key words).

compliant and reduces the administrative burden for the IT organization. Using existing technology has a number benefits including:

- Minimal deployment costs in terms of training, additional licenses, etc.
- Scalable architecture, extensible and compatible with current applications
- Reduced training cost

Essentially, aligning the compliance solution with current procedures and existing technology can reduce the cost of compliance and improve the return on investment for existing application.

Building an Integrated, Long-Term Compliance Solution

Integrated, long-term compliance solutions provide a flexible and adaptable architecture that addresses immediate compliance needs while facilitating ongoing compliance management. Future compliance planning should integrate products from all vendors to help the enterprise extend its compliance solutions. Future solutions will focus on the following areas:

- Document life-cycle management
- Storage
- E-mail compliance
- Workflow management
- Business intelligence
- Financial analytics

Industry Partner Support

Long-term compliance solutions require a broad partner ecosystem, including telcos and audio conference providers, independent software vendors, systems integrators, and accounting firms, to support specific compliance needs:

- *Accounting firms offer critical compliance expertise.* Many accounting firms have rich content libraries for supporting compliance. Your enterprise compliance solutions should be compatible with the libraries of your current auditors as well as industry standards such as Ernst & Young LLP, PricewaterhouseCoopers, KPMG International, and Deloitte & Touche LLP.

- *Telcos and audio conference providers.* Leading telcos and audio conference providers like MCI, BT, and InterCall offer audio conference call controls to enhance collaboration and information exchange.

- *Solution integrators provide technical support and customer interface.* Technical support, including integration and enhancement, is essential to scale effectively and improve compliance efficiency.

- *Independent software vendors deliver value-adding functionality.* Complementary vendors will be able to fill gaps for expanded functionality in areas such as business intelligence and records management.

Summary

External audit requirements of most compliance regulations such as SOX, plus legal and commercial consequences of noncompliance, are motivating executives to mitigate noncompliance risks. Managing compliance can involve a large, multidisciplinary compliance team working together within a complex legal, financial, and IT framework. Challenges include distributed people, systems, and data, plus undefined taxonomies and lack of best practices. Real-time collaboration solutions are becoming a key part of a comprehensive long-term response to corporate compliance needs. Collaboration and instant communication contributes to work speed and quality, lower program cost, and lower overall risk of noncompliance—adding immediacy to how compliance teams succeed.

Managing the Cost of Compliance

We have spent a good deal of time talking about the cost of non-compliance and the need to enable compliance and provide solid guidance. It is worth some time to glance at the cost of enablement. Gartner Group's Daryl Plummer stated in December of 2005 that, "As international commerce regulations increase, spending on regulatory compliance is growing at a rate twice that of IT spending."[1]

AMR Research, in 2005, noted that "companies expected to spend $5.8 billion to meet SOX requirements in 2005. And while technology spending represents just 28% of the overall budget, it's increasing by the largest percentage—up 43% from $1.13 billion in 2004 to $1.62 billion in 2005."[2]

The estimates for building and managing compliance systems are high but in light of the losses from the corporate corrupt practices failures we have discussed, these costs are likely to continue as a fact of life. Looking to technology as a means of driving efficient and effective support for compliance is not only reasonable but imperative.

Chapter Summary

Governance and compliance is complex because of the growing landscape of rules and their impact on execution and the need for transparent scrutiny. By managing the codification, usage, and measurement of compliance rules that need to continually adapt to the complexities of business, an organization is provided with the foundation for protecting brand reputation, while at the same time creating new levels of trust and fairness to all.

Eric Hoffer, the philosopher and author, once described the difference between learning and knowing by stating that:

> The learners will inherit the Earth, while the knowers will find themselves beautifully equipped to deal with a world that no longer exists.

As we move further into the global economy, enterprises need to be "Learners" rather than mere "Knowers." Rather than cobble together security, authentication, and encryption solutions to enable their workers to continue to use twentieth-century means of communications, such as physical and electronic mail, it makes more sense for them to migrate to a collaboration and interactive environment. In addition to gaining increased return on investment (ROI) and reduced total cost of ownership (TCO) as a result of this migration, enterprises should find that they are better able to adopt a holistic, enterprise-wide compliance program. Such a proactive approach is becoming a necessity as a result of a blizzard of regulations requiring the review, archiving, production, and audit of business records that include instant messaging. It also may be advisable in light of:

- The regulatory trend toward accelerated reporting deadlines.
- An increased emphasis on enterprise-wide communication and collaboration.
- The need for companies to establish an "effective compliance and ethics program." Requiring an ecosystem-wide capability for an environment designed to help "Learner" enterprises stay ahead of the regulatory compliance curve.

Few businesses can afford ad hoc compliance programs. The number and scope of compliance regulations have increased dramatically over the last few years, making compliance an ever-complex business and technology challenge. Whether aimed to prevent fraud and money laundering, to combat international terrorism, or to ensure financial accountability and privacy, a kaleidoscope of international, federal, and state regulations—such as the USA PATRIOT Act, Sarbanes-Oxley, Basel II, Bank of England, Bank Secrecy Act, HIPAA, and others—dramatically impacts how companies do business.

To be successful, organizations serious about compliance must also be serious about data quality because at the core of any reliable compliance program is quality data. Ideally, an organization's compliance software will provide specialized data quality and matching capabilities as part of an all-encompassing enterprise compliance and case management solution.

Organizations that have pieced together their compliance process should carefully review its design and audit its results to ensure that the process that has developed over time is up to the task of meeting the company's current requirements. In particular, organizations that plan to use existing data quality software for their compliance efforts must carefully examine the software's ability to effectively extend its rules and processing capabilities in order to provide mission-critical and compliance-specific capabilities, without which the entire compliance process could be undermined.

Notes

1. Daryl Plummer, "Gartner Predicts: The Cost of Compliance," webcast by Gartner Group, December 2005.
2. Chris Egizi, "The High Cost of Compliance," IBM CIO Update, March 11, 2005.

Sarbanes-Oxley Act of 2002—Effective Compliance and Ethics Program

The sections included here have been referenced throughout this book and are provided for your reference. They set forth the requirements for an effective compliance and ethics program.

The full act can be obtained from the U.S. government web sites or directly by contacting any number of government agencies, including the Small Business Administration and the Department of Commerce.

§8B2.1. Effective Compliance and Ethics Program

(a) To have an effective compliance and ethics program, for purposes of subsection (f) of §8C2.5 (Culpability Score) and subsection (c)(1) of §8D1.4 (Recommended Conditions of Probation–Organizations), an organization shall—

1. exercise due diligence to prevent and detect criminal conduct; and

2. otherwise promote an organizational culture that encourages ethical conduct and a commitment to compliance with the law.

Such compliance and ethics program shall be reasonably designed, implemented, and enforced so that the program is generally effective in preventing and detecting criminal conduct. The failure to prevent or detect the instant offense does not necessarily mean that the program is not generally effective in preventing and detecting criminal conduct.

(b) Due diligence and the promotion of an organizational culture that encourages ethical conduct and a commitment to compliance with the law within the meaning of subsection (a) minimally require the following:

1. The organization shall establish standards and procedures to prevent and detect criminal conduct.

2. **(a)** The organization's governing authority shall be knowledgeable about the content and operation of the compliance and ethics program and shall exercise reasonable

oversight with respect to the implementation and effectiveness of the compliance and ethics program.

(b) High-level personnel of the organization shall ensure that the organization has an effective compliance and ethics program, as described in this guideline. Specific individual(s) within high-level personnel shall be assigned overall responsibility for the compliance and ethics program.

(c) Specific individual(s) within the organization shall be delegated day-to-day operational responsibility for the compliance and ethics program. Individual(s) with operational responsibility shall report periodically to high-level personnel and, as appropriate, to the governing authority, or an appropriate subgroup of the governing authority, on the effectiveness of the compliance and ethics program. To carry out such operational responsibility, such individual(s) shall be given adequate resources, appropriate authority, and direct access to the governing authority or an appropriate subgroup of the governing authority.

3. The organization shall use reasonable efforts not to include within the substantial authority personnel of the organization any individual whom the organization knew, or should have known through the exercise of due diligence, has engaged in illegal activities or other conduct inconsistent with an effective compliance and ethics program.

4. (a) The organization shall take reasonable steps to communicate periodically and in a practical manner its standards and procedures, and other aspects of the compliance and ethics program, to the individuals referred to in subdivision (B) by conducting effective training programs and otherwise disseminating information appropriate to such individuals' respective roles and responsibilities.

(b) The individuals referred to in subdivision (A) are the members of the governing authority, high-level personnel, substantial authority personnel, the organization's employees, and, as appropriate, the organization's agents.

5. The organization shall take reasonable steps—

(a) to ensure that the organization's compliance and ethics program is followed, including monitoring and auditing to detect criminal conduct;

(b) to evaluate periodically the effectiveness of the organization's compliance and ethics program; and

(c) to have and publicize a system, which may include mechanisms that allow for anonymity or confidentiality, whereby the organization's employees and agents may report or seek guidance regarding potential or actual criminal conduct without fear of retaliation.

6. The organization's compliance and ethics program shall be promoted and enforced consistently throughout the organization through (A) appropriate incentives to perform in accordance with the compliance and ethics program; and (B) appropriate disciplinary measures for engaging in criminal conduct and for failing to take reasonable steps to prevent or detect criminal conduct.

7. After criminal conduct has been detected, the organization shall take reasonable steps to respond appropriately to the criminal conduct and to prevent further similar criminal conduct, including making any necessary modifications to the organization's compliance and ethics program.

(c) In implementing subsection (b), the organization shall periodically assess the risk of criminal conduct and shall take appropriate steps to design, implement, or modify each requirement set forth in subsection (b) to reduce the risk of criminal conduct identified through this process.

Commentary Application Notes:

1. Definitions—For purposes of this guideline:

"Compliance and ethics program" means a program designed to prevent and detect criminal conduct.

"Governing authority" means the (A) the Board of Directors; or (B) if the organization does not have a Board of Directors, the highest-level governing body of the organization.

"High-level personnel of the organization" and "substantial authority personnel" have the meaning given those terms in the Commentary to §8A1.2 (Application Instructions-Organizations).

"Standards and procedures" means standards of conduct and internal controls that are reasonably capable of reducing the likelihood of criminal conduct.

2. Factors to Consider in Meeting Requirements of This Guideline:

(a) In General—Each of the requirements set forth in this guideline shall be met by an organization; however, in determining what specific actions are necessary to meet those requirements, factors that shall be considered include: (i) applicable industry practice or the standards called for by any applicable governmental regulation; (ii) the size of the organization; and (iii) similar misconduct.

(b) Applicable Governmental Regulation and Industry Practice— An organization's failure to incorporate and follow applicable industry practice or the standards called for by any applicable governmental regulation weighs against a finding of an effective compliance and ethics program.

(c) The Size of the Organization:

i. In General—The formality and scope of actions that an organization shall take to meet the requirements of this guideline, including the necessary features of the organization's standards and procedures, depend on the size of the organization.

ii. Large Organizations—A large organization generally shall devote more formal operations and greater resources in meeting the requirements of this guideline than shall a small organization. As appropriate, a large organization should encourage small organizations (especially those that have, or seek to have, a business relationship with the large organization) to implement effective compliance and ethics programs.

iii. Small Organizations—In meeting the requirements of this guideline, small organizations shall demonstrate the same degree of commitment to ethical conduct and compliance with the law as large organizations. However, a small organization may meet the requirements of this guideline with less formality and fewer resources than would be expected of large organizations. In appropriate circumstances, reliance on existing resources and simple systems can demonstrate a degree of commitment that, for a large organization, would only be demonstrated through more formally planned and implemented systems.

Examples of the informality and use of fewer resources with which a small organization may meet the requirements of this guideline include the following: (I) the governing authority's discharge of its responsibility for oversight of the compliance and ethics program by directly managing the organization's compliance and ethics efforts; (II) training employees through informal staff meetings, and monitoring through regular "walk-arounds" or continuous observation while managing the organization; (III) using available personnel, rather than employing separate staff, to carry out the compliance and ethics program; and (IV) modeling its own compliance and ethics program on existing, well-regarded compliance and ethics programs and best practices of other similar organizations.

(d) Recurrence of Similar Misconduct—Recurrence of similar misconduct creates doubt regarding whether the organization took reasonable steps to meet the requirements of this guideline. For purposes of this subdivision, "similar misconduct" has the meaning given that term in the Commentary to §8A1.2 (Application Instructions–Organizations).

3. Application of Subsection (b)(2).

High-level personnel and substantial authority personnel of the organization shall be knowledgeable about the content and operation of the compliance and ethics program, shall perform their assigned duties consistent with the exercise of due diligence, and shall promote an organizational culture that encourages ethical conduct and a commitment to compliance with the law.

If the specific individual(s) assigned overall responsibility for the compliance and ethics program does not have day-to-day operational responsibility for the program, then the individual(s) with day-to-day operational responsibility for the program typically should, no less than annually, give the governing authority or an appropriate subgroup thereof information on the implementation and effectiveness of the compliance and ethics program.

4. Application of Subsection (b)(3):

(a) Consistency with Other Law—Nothing in subsection (b)(3) is intended to require conduct inconsistent with any Federal, State, or local law, including any law governing employment or hiring practices.

(b) Implementation—In implementing subsection (b)(3), the organization shall hire and promote individuals so as to ensure that all individuals within the high-level personnel and substantial authority personnel of the organization will perform their assigned duties in a manner consistent with the exercise of due diligence and the promotion of an organizational culture that encourages ethical conduct and a commitment to compliance with the law under subsection (a). With respect to the hiring or promotion of such individuals, an organization shall consider the relatedness of the individual's illegal activities and other misconduct (i.e., other conduct inconsistent with an effective compliance and ethics program) to the specific responsibilities the individual is anticipated to be assigned and other factors such as: (i) the recency of the individual's illegal activities and other misconduct; and (ii) whether the individual has engaged in other such illegal activities and other such misconduct.

5. Application of Subsection (b)(6).

Adequate discipline of individuals responsible for an offense is a necessary component of enforcement; however, the form of discipline that will be appropriate will be case specific.

6. Application of Subsection (c).

To meet the requirements of subsection (c), an organization shall:

(a) Assess periodically the risk that criminal conduct will occur, including assessing the following:

  i. The nature and seriousness of such criminal conduct.

ii. The likelihood that certain criminal conduct may occur because of the nature of the organization's business. If, because of the nature of an organization's business, there is a substantial risk that certain types of criminal conduct may occur, the organization shall take reasonable steps to prevent and detect that type of criminal conduct. For example, an organization that, due to the nature of its business, employs sales personnel who have flexibility to set prices shall establish standards and procedures designed to prevent and detect price-fixing. An organization that, due to the nature of its business, employs sales personnel who have flexibility to represent the material characteristics of a product shall establish standards and procedures designed to prevent and detect fraud.

iii. The prior history of the organization. The prior history of an organization may indicate types of criminal conduct that it shall take actions to prevent and detect.

(b) Prioritize periodically, as appropriate, the actions taken pursuant to any requirement set forth in subsection (b), in order to focus on preventing and detecting the criminal conduct identified under subdivision (A) of this note as most serious, and most likely, to occur.

(c) Modify, as appropriate, the actions taken pursuant to any requirement set forth in subsection (b) to reduce the risk of criminal conduct identified under subdivision (A) of this note as most serious, and most likely, to occur.

Background: This section sets forth the requirements for an effective compliance and ethics program. This section responds to section 805(a)(2)(5) of the Sarbanes-Oxley Act of 2002, Public Law 107–204, which directed the Commission to review and amend, as appropriate, the guidelines and related policy statements to ensure that the guidelines that apply to organizations in this chapter "are sufficient to deter and punish organizational criminal misconduct."

The requirements set forth in this guideline are intended to achieve reasonable prevention and detection of criminal conduct for which the organization would be vicariously liable. The prior diligence of an organization in seeking to prevent and detect criminal conduct has a direct bearing on the appropriate penalties and probation terms for the organization if it is convicted and sentenced for a criminal offense.

Historical Note: Effective November 1, 2004

Description of the Technology Features Relevant to Compliance

The following table describes the technology features that are relevant to regulatory compliance. This table is provided as a summary reference for the features and technologies referenced earlier in this book. It is not an exhaustive list but is intended as a summary of our discussion.

Feature-to-Compliance Mapping

Feature	Confidentiality	Integrity	Availability	Procedural Rigor	Auditing and Logging
Web content management (WCM)			X	X	
Enterprise search			X		
Document and records management	X	X	X	X	X
Auditing and logging	X	X		X	X
Records center	X	X	X	X	X
Information rights management (IRM)	X	X			
Document policies	X	X		X	
Extensible hold and content expiration infrastructure			X	X	
Role-based targeting and security	X	X		X	
Custom workflows			X	X	
Custom notifications			X	X	
Custom tasks				X	
Data aggregation and reporting			X		

Workflow processes		X	X	
E-mail messages and alerts		X	X	
Content types	X	X	X	
Search		X	X	X
Versioning and history	X		X	
Document metadata	X	X	X	
List-level and item-level security	X		X	X
Instant Messaging (IM) session history		X		X
Encrypted messaging	X			
Secure communications	X			
Secure e-mail message repository		X		X
Permission control	X	X	X	
Message classification		X		X
Transport rules	X		X	
Secure communications	X			
Classified e-mail	X			
Information Rights Management (IRM)	X			

(Continued)

Feature-to-Compliance Mapping

Feature	Confidentiality	Integrity	Availability	Procedural Rigor	Auditing and Logging
E-mail records management			X		X
E-mail search			X		X
Secure communications	X				
Spreadsheet integrity		X			
Spreadsheet archiving and centralization			X		X
Role-based views and access control	X	X			
Data security	X				
Sarbanes-Oxley (SOX) templates		X		X	
ISO 9001 templates				X	
Finance and accounting templates				X	
Feedback monitoring				X	
Report preparation		X		X	
Forms archiving and centralization			X	X	
Data validation		X			
Custom development and extensibility				X	X

Index

Index

Index

Index

Index